GROUPWORK IN ADOPTION
AND FOSTER CARE

Child Care Policy and Practice Series
General Editor: Tony Hall
Director and Secretary
British Agencies for Adoption and Fostering

GROUPWORK IN ADOPTION AND FOSTER CARE

Edited by
JOHN TRISELIOTIS

B.T. Batsford Ltd · *London*
in association with
British Agencies for Adoption and Fostering

First published 1988
All rights reserved. No part of this publication may be
reproduced, in any form or by any means, without permission
from the publisher
Typeset by Progress Filmsetting Ltd
and printed and bound in Great Britain by
Biddles Ltd
Guildford and Kings Lynn
Published by B.T. Batsford Ltd
4 Fitzhardinge Street, London W1H 0AH

British Library Cataloguing in Publication Data

Groupwork in adoption and foster care.—
  (Child care policy and practice).
  1. Adoption — Great Britain   2. Foster
  home care — Great Britain
  I. Triseliotis, John   II. Series
  362.7'33'0941   HV875.7.G7

  ISBN 0–7134–5459–8
  ISBN 0–7134–5460–1 Pbk

CONTENTS

ACKNOWLEDGEMENTS

This book arose out of enquiries by many students and a number of practitioners wanting to know more about the use of groups in adoption and foster care. A number of people through their efforts and suggestions helped to make its compilation possible and I am greatly indebted to them. They are: Joan Fratter, Senior Social Worker with Barnardo's Homefinding Project in Barkingside; Gerry O'Hara, Regional Officer, Children and Families, Lothian Region; Paul Wearing, Project Leader with Barnardo's in Edinburgh; and John Hodge, Lecturer in Social Work at the University of Newcastle. I should also like to express very many thanks to the various secretaries who did the typing.

THE CONTRIBUTORS

JANA BROWN was a part-time Fostering Officer and part-time Social Work Liaison Officer at the University of East Anglia.

OTTIS EDWARDS is a Social Worker attached to the Adoption and Fostering team, Lambeth Borough.

CHRIS FINES is the Director of Parents for Children, London.

CECILY GRIFFITH is a Social Worker, Adoption and Fostering Team, Lambeth Borough.

MARJORIE HELM is a Project Social Worker with the Family Placement Project at Barnardo's in Newcastle Upon Tyne.

PAULINE HOGGAN is a Regional Co-ordinator – Adoption and Fostering, Lothian Region.

SANDRA HUTTON is an adoptive parent and secretary to the Lothian Adopters' Group.

BERYL JEFFERIES is a Team Leader attached to the Adoption and Fostering team, Lambeth Borough.

DICK O'BRIEN is a Community Care Co-ordinator with Central Region.

GERRY O'HARA is a Regional Officer – Children and Families with Lothian Region.

AUDREY MULLENDER is a Lecturer in Social Work at the University of Nottingham and was a consultant to the Ebony foster parent group.

SYLVIA MURPHY was a Project Social Worker with the Family Placement Project at Barnardo's North East Division. She is currently a Senior Social Worker with West Sussex Social Service Department.

CAROLE SMITH was formerly a Project Leader for Barnardo's, Yorkshire Division, Homefinding Unit and for the past five years she has been Unit Leader for the Fostering and Adoption Unit of Kirklees Metropolitan Council.

JOHN TRISELIOTIS is the Director of Social Work Education at the University of Edinburgh.

General Introduction

This volume sets out to examine and provide examples of recent practice initiatives which have contributed to the development of groupwork practice in the fields of adoption and foster care in both statutory and voluntary social work agencies. The wider use of groupwork techniques and strategies in this field has been mainly in three ways: to prepare and train would-be foster and adoptive parents; to prepare children before they move to new families or to independent living; or as a means for offering post-placement support.

The wisdom of concentrating on preparatory and post-placement work is increasingly being confirmed by empirical studies, to be referred to later, which claim an association between such work, greater placement stability and fewer placement breakdowns.

Historical background

For historical reasons the use of groups in social work had been neglected over a long period, though in recent years it seems to be experiencing a 'rebirth', at least in relation to certain client groups. The historical forces which appear to have held back developments were largely associated with the rise of psychoanalysis and its influence on casework techniques. If the settlement movement at the end of the last century was a demonstration of concern for community and neighbour-hood development through stimulating activity type groups, psychoanalysis, with its attention on the individual in relative isolation from his social environment, was a move in the opposite direction. As a result activity groups with adult or youth or educational type groups came to be undervalued and were seen as detracting from the pursuit of proper 'professional' objectives. Douglas (1978) laments that 'this concentration on the individual and his behaviour has left us very few inclinations or abilities to respond to the crying need to understand the ways in which the groups, of which we are a part, have such an important influence on our lives'.

Though Mary Richmond, writing before the impact of psychoanalysis on social work (1920, p. 256) was very welcoming towards what she described as 'the new tendency to view our clients from the angle of what might be termed small group psychology', Schwartz (1971) comments on how the paths of individual and small group preoccupation diverged after the 1920s and went their separate ways, which led Linderman to complain that he could not see why 'groups and group experience do not stand at the very centre of social work's concern' (1939, p. 344).

It was only in the early 1970s that both here and in the USA, in the words of Schwartz (1971, p. 4) 'the group experience has indeed begun to move closer to the centre of social work's concern'. The rebirth of interest in small groups, as we shall see later, owed less to the influence of psychotherapy type groups, which were the dominant model at the time, and much more to the initiatives of some social workers who began to use groups as the natural response to some of their clients' needs. These initiatives took place mainly in the fields of community work, juvenile delinquency and child care and were mostly a direct result of agency function. Brown et al. (1982) saw this new move as having emerged not so much through the influence of 'educators', researchers or theoreticians, but as a means of working devised and developed by practitioners employed in statutory agencies.

Group psychotherapy, as described and practised by people such as Jones (1953), Slavson (1956), Bion (1961) and Walton (1971), derived its theoretical underpinning mainly from psychoanalysis, and as a model of groupwork practice, it had considerable influence on social work with groups. The leadership method employed by this approach was mostly passive and the techniques used non-directive, relying largely on the interpretation of here and now phenomena occurring in the group, or to here and then interpretations of material shared by individual members. Gestalt, encounter and Rogerian groups were other variants of group psychotherapy that dominated social work thinking, if not practice. The fact that social workers were unable to transfer or adapt these predominantly clinical models in their essentially social settings seemed beyond the point but it resulted in a kind of paralysis on the group work front.

Understanding the emotional forces present within groups is an essential skill of all group workers, but only a few social workers will ever find themselves in situations where their primary task is either one in which they are asked to study group behaviour or use the group for exclusively therapeutic purposes in the way described above. A further problem was the failure to separate the theory from the methods. While a number of theories, particularly from humanistic psychology, can offer valuable insights into human behaviour and into the functioning of groups, application has to take account of both setting and need and the methods adapted accordingly. For instance, styles of leadership and techniques applied in the treatment of mentally ill people in the relative safety of an institution could prove damaging to some clients of social work, e.g. acting out offenders.

It was against this background of relative frustration and inactivity that wider changes in social work were to stimulate new thinking among practitioners on how to respond to needs for which the predominant models of the period had little to offer. The new forces included the reorganization of social work in 1970 resulting in workers having to respond to a range of new needs. The search for alternative methods was stimulated particularly by the rise of community work and by new ideas surrounding the fields of community care and the diversion of young offenders from corrective institutions. It was mainly in these new fields that most initial experimentation of a new type of groupwork was developed. Developmental, action or self-help-type groups began to appear in these fields with examples such as tenants' associations, claimants' unions and self-help groups for the parents of handicapped children or for the disabled. Ideas for diverting children from custodial sentences built into the Children and Young Person's Act, 1969, led to the setting up of intermediate treatment groups (I.T.) aiming to combine care and control for mostly involuntary clients on supervision from the courts. Brown et al. (1982) also put the emphasis for the new wider developments in groupwork down to 'practice wisdom' adding that the theoretical concepts informing the new model of groupwork practice came from several directions. In some types of group, they add, leaders may make psychodynamic interpretations 'when these are thought useful for improving personal or group functioning', whilst role-play, 'homework' and reinforcement are typical behavioural elements. An emphasis on feelings, 'getting in touch with one's self', self disclosure and the acceptance of self, reflect a Rogerian influence. Systems concepts are implied by explorations of the effect on the group and individual members of the outside environment. These developments, in the authors' views, suggest the emergence of an eclectic groupwork model where the theoretical orientation, far from being prescribed, is dictated by the purpose of the group and the kind of need it is trying to address.

It is becoming increasingly obvious that the multifarious needs social workers are trying to address and the different types of groups required to respond to these cannot be informed by a single theoretical perspective or be reduced to a single model of practice. The 'new' approach, as it has been called, tries to identify the kind of theory that best explains the needs of the particular group under discussion and then to use the group approach that gives most promise of achieving the desired objectives.

The use of groups in adoption and foster care

Like other recent developments in the use of groups in social work, developments in the field of adoption and foster care have also been largely a response to agency function and to needs that were either new or had previously gone unnoticed. Some of the new ideas had to do with the requirements of what came to be known as 'special need' children, along with new thinking about diverting children from custodial sentences and from institutional living and integrating them with the community.

The groups that were developed in the fields of adoption and foster care appear to have borrowed their ideas mostly from the fields of education, concerning adult learning and training; from sociology, in relation to role performance; and ideas connected with task performance and skill development from social learning theory. For example, Kirk's writings (1964 and 1970) with their stress on 'role' performance and 'educative' processes were influential in the approach increasingly adopted for the preparation and evaluation of adoptive and foster parents through small groups. Equally, the use of groups for preparing children before they move to new families, owes much to the influence of I.T. groups which, in turn, were largely based on ideas from education and behavioural psychology. Yet it is unlikely that these ideas would have had their impact had it not been for the changing nature of adoption and foster care from the 1970s onwards.

There are only a few examples, mostly American, describing the exploratory use of groups in this field of child care, which go back to the 1960s. Stanley (1963) gives an account of using group meetings in Florida as a way of studying foster homes in preference to traditional methods. Dillow (1971) also describes a group approach as part of the preparation and assessment of adoptive parents. A couple of examples can also be found of time-limited support groups being set up for existing foster parents as part of a policy of 'caring for the carers' (Mills et al. 1967). During the same period, groups were also used to offer children in care the opportunity to reflect on their 'in care' or foster care status, but not as part of an explicit policy to prepare them for new families (Watson and Boverman 1971, Peterson and Sturgies 1971). These were examples of well-structured, time-limited and task-centred groups. Only a couple of isolated examples exist of similar work being undertaken in Britain (McWhinnie 1968, Ball and Bailey 1969). The latter does not seem to have been well thought through before it started.

A common model

Though each type of group described here has its distinctive characteristics, nevertheless a common model also emerges from the way all three types are being run. All of the groups are:

(i) Well structured.

(ii) Task-centred with a clear and specific purpose in mind, e.g. the preparation of foster and adoptive parents, or the preparation of children before they move. Such broad objectives are subsequently broken into smaller specific tasks. (What is done in groups is meant to link closely with work at the individual level.) Douglas (1986, p. 112) claims from a review of the literature that, where groups are engaged with a clear-cut task, then members 'are task oriented, less aggressive, and more involved than members of groups with ambiguous tasks'.

(iii) Contractual in nature – all parties reach agreement on the objectives to be pursued.

(iv) Topic-orientated – a kind of curriculum is prepared and each session is focused on a relevant theme, issue or problem, e.g. the place of the natural family in the child's life or the clarification of the fostering role.

(v) Time-limited, with 6–8 sessions for the accomplishment of the task. (Post-placement support groups are usually more open-ended.)

(vi) The method is a combination of discussion, problem solving, information giving, activity and education. It demonstrates a definite departure from past groupwork in that it aims to integrate 'talking' and 'discussion' with activities, compared to discussion only. Schulman (1971) bases his arguments for combining 'talking' and 'doing' on the idea that people communicate and learn through a variety of mediums – words, facial and body expressions, touch and shared experiences of various kinds and that these transactions cannot be categorized into 'talking' and 'doing'.

Some underlying assumptions

There are a number of underlying assumptions informing the use of groups in this aspect of child care work. Some of these are increasingly being supported by empirical studies. The primary assumption is that children who cannot live with their parents, either temporarily or permanently, require preparation before they move to new families. Similarly, that the families who undertake this task require preparation, training and post-placement support to enable them to fulfil their temporary or permanent parenting role. More important, that groups are an effective and appropriate means of contributing to the achievement of such goals. Claims made for the use of groups include the following: people can learn from each other and the workers; groups offer opportunities for members to help each other; to reduce feelings of being vetted or investigated among prospective adoptive and foster parents; thoughts and feelings related to the task of the group can be more easily shared with those who have similar concerns; attitude changes are more easily achieved; the performance of new roles and tasks which require preparation and learning can more easily be achieved through discussion and information exchange than in individual contacts; activity, as a medium, can help in the acquisition of the new skills; and finally that readiness to assume new roles and responsibilities in relation to children can be better assessed through groups.

The contributions

The contributions in this volume are divided into three sections covering the use of groups in three distinct areas of child care work.

They are:
(i)   The preparation and selection of adoptive and foster parents;
(ii)   Using groups to prepare and support children;
(iii) Post-placement and post-adoptive support groups.

Section 1

The preparation and selection of adoptive and foster parents

1

Introduction

John Triseliotis

Social workers involved in finding adoptive or foster homes are constantly faced with the difficult task of identifying families that will provide a certain standard of care for children needing a new family. The job becomes more complicated and uncertain when it is recognized that there is no agreed recipe for being a 'good' parent and no established criteria against which to measure acceptability for the adoptive or foster care role. There are many definitions of the 'healthy' or 'well-functioning' family, based mostly on studies of American families which may not necessarily hold true of families elsewhere.

Past studies provided some guidelines about the kind of characteristics associated with successful adoption or fostering, but these have not yet fully caught up with the more recent developments. The adoption of special needs children and 'specialist' or contract fostering are not the same as the adoption of infants or the fostering of children mostly needing care. Furthermore, it is argued that some of the couples who seem successful in 'parenting' special needs children would have been rejected by agencies 15–20 years ago, the argument being that it takes atypical people to parent special needs children. In other words, there are many different kinds of people who can care for special needs children and children may do particularly well with what are seen as 'unconventional' families. No agency has yet said though that every person can be a psychological parent to a child.

The emphasis on preparation and training

It is mainly because of all the uncertainties in identifying suitable criteria for carers to parent (particularly special needs) children, that agencies have begun to put the emphasis on the preparation of would-be adoptive and foster carers rather than simply concentrating on selection with no firm criteria in mind and no standardized ways of identifying the qualities sought. It was also becoming obvious from a number of studies and from practice experience that adoptive and foster parents were mostly critical of many aspects of traditional home study approaches (Bradley 1966, Goodacre 1966). Applicants for the adoptive or foster care role used to experience the selection process, based mostly on individual interviews, as too intrusive, with themselves as suspects having to prove their suitability. There was hostility and resentment at what some described as the 'inquisitorial' approach of some social workers and the inexplicitness about how information was interpreted and assessed. Worse, negative feelings were generated by the vague reasons offered for refusing couples. Goodacre (1966) commented that most adopters tried to make the impression they thought would be most favourable to their applications. Even as recently as 1984, Macaskill concluded from her study of families who applied to adopt mentally handicapped children, that formal interviews tended to obscure the families' true potential and did not offer them the opportunity to show their practical expertise.

It was within this climate of dissatisfaction that Kirk's ideas (1964) of an alternative approach appeared. In his book and in subsequent seminars in Britain (1970), Kirk put forward the idea of using 'a group educative' approach as a method of 'self-selection' and of preparing would-be adopters (and by extension foster carers). We will see later, how developments during the next fifteen or so years followed or departed from Kirk's expectations and how the ideas were adapted to suit agency function and the perceived needs of clients. Kirk's ideas for the adoption of a 'group educative' approach were only very gradually taken up. Before the 1970s only a couple of examples were available from the USA describing the use of preparatory groups and none, as far as could be established, from Britain.

The real pressure for change in Britain, and also in the USA, came from the changing nature of foster care and adoption in the 1970s and the different type of child now being put forward for placement. Social workers were no longer dealing with either 'perfect' babies to be placed with the 'perfect' family, nor with mostly young and trouble-free children to go into foster homes. The need now was for foster carers and adopters who would be able to respond to the needs of older children, some of whom might be physically or mentally handicapped or display behaviour and/or emotional problems. Two new factors were now dominating the child care scene: that of special needs children requiring new families, and ideas about 'normalization' and 'community care' in relation to delinquent children previously sent to residential institutions. Both gave rise to appeals for adoptive and foster parents to take on a challenging child care job.

Selection or self-selection

The emergence of these new needs was placing different demands on social workers and carers compared to the past and it was beginning to suggest groups as a key medium of communication. Groups were gradually being seen as a vehicle for the transmission of information and ideas, the preparation of carers for different parenting tasks and for supporting carers to carry out these tasks. The use of preparatory groups is based on the premise that many applicants are ignorant of what is involved in parenting someone else's child and would benefit from information and exploration of ideas. Furthermore, that they offer to applicants the opportunity to explore their readiness and discover their strengths and weaknesses for the task ahead. Hazel (1981) who was one of the first to use groups in this field in Britain saw them as an instrument for the selection of foster families and as 'people helping each other'. She defined the process as 'offering applicants the opportunity of discovering for themselves, by attendance at group meetings, whether it was the kind of work they really wanted to do. Also whether they had the necessary aptitudes and facility for it, with guidance from other group members.' Though she described the process as one of 'self-selection', she qualified it by adding that 'self-selection' was limited by the social worker's role as 'match-maker'. At about the same time as Hazel, a number of adoption agencies were also beginning to experiment in using groups for the preparation and/or selection of would-be adopters.

The use of groups in this area of child care practice has highlighted both the potential of groups, and some of the ambiguities surrounding their objectives. In the first place, and unlike Kirk's (1964) original ideas, there is no evidence that any agency has put all its reliance on groups, abandoning the individual home study. Agencies seem to combine the two approaches. A more difficult conceptual issue is how far the group is simply preparatory in nature, leading to 'self-selection', or whether assessment elements enter into its process. With the exception of Smith's contribution here, the other contributors, whilst putting emphasis on education and preparation, nevertheless use observations at group meetings in varying degrees to aid assessment and selection. Experience so far suggests that, though a number of applicants will eventually select themselves out by withdrawing from groups, this is not always the case. Group leaders, aware of the agency's responsibility to safeguard the interests of the children, are prepared to share observations from the group process with the workers carrying out the home study.

The issue of whether groups are meant to be preparatory in nature or a combination of education, preparation and assessment is relevant also in relation to the timing of the home study. If groups are meant to be preparatory, to offer participants the opportunity to learn and perhaps adapt their attitudes, then it stands to reason that the home study should commence at the end of preparation. Yet practice seems to vary, with most agencies starting the home study simultaneously or mid-way through the group sessions. Leaving the home study till the end might equally elicit complaints from applicants about unreasonable delays.

Task orientation

The examples provided in this section illustrate a predominantly task-centred approach in the use of groups. Each group has to accomplish a number of tasks which have been identified as relevant in the performance of the adoptive or fostering role. Participants are expected to work at tasks as a way of learning about the adoptive and fostering roles and the handling of potentially problematic situations. As already mentioned, such groups are different from those where the focus is on relationships with treatment objectives in mind. The tasks identified in the former groups have educative aspects about them and cover such areas as: child development; understanding the needs of separated children; the place of the family of origin in the child's life and self-concept; the handling of difficult behaviour; and the part played by the agency and the role of the professionals. In the case of foster parents, particular emphasis is placed on role definition, on expectations and on working relationships between social workers and foster carers. Groups are ideally suited to introduce would-be foster parents to: the nature of the foster care task; the complexity of roles and relationships surrounding fostering; the different types of fostering, placing different expectations on foster carers; the idea of contract; the place of the natural family; the relationship between the foster parents, the social worker and the agency; and issues of responsibility, authority and accountability. A reasonable conclusion to be drawn from Chapter 9 of the Beckford Inquiry (1986) is that the lack of clarity and the ambiguity surrounding the areas outlined above contributed to the tragedy.

Cognitive v experiential processes

In the early phase of using task-orientated groups, the pattern was to invite mostly outside 'experts' to speak to the group on the topics or tasks identified earlier and then to have discussion. Organizers though were soon to recognize, as Fines points out here, what other educators had found before, i.e. that people learn in different ways, ranging from the cognitive to the more experiential approach.

As a result, the approach has decidedly shifted from being predominantly cognitive and passive to becoming more experiential. More emphasis is placed now on participants sharing and exploring their own ideas and experiences on the same tasks, exposing their knowledge, attitudes and sometimes ignorance and prejudices. Group members are encouraged to share feelings and fears, to discover their strengths and weaknesses and generally to learn from each other. Input by people who have adopted or fostered introduces a touch of reality to abstract discussions and hypothetical situations. Outside speakers and audio-visual aids play a part but a more minor one.

Group composition

Preparing to set up such groups does not differ from that for any other type of group. The readiness and willingness of people to participate is still important and decisions have to be made about time and place of meetings, desirable numbers, rules about attendance and confidentiality. The composition of the groups is one that seems to raise a number of questions, particularly how homogeneous or heterogeneous they should be. For example, should there be a mix of those with children with childless or single applicants; of the articulate with the less so; of those who wish to adopt or foster adolescents or handicapped children with the rest? Should adoptive and foster applicants be in mixed or separate groups? Concerning the latter issue, while it is recognized that there are many overlaps between adoption and foster care, nevertheless there are also many distinct and important differences between the two. Confusion over this can lead to false or distorted expectations and perhaps distress all round. With regard to the other issues though, most workers seem to go for heterogeneity and in this they are supported by group theory. Whilst some commonality of need seems necessary, Reddy (1977) and Smith (1974) found empirical evidence supporting the view that when group membership consists of some persons who are high on a particular need and others low on that same need, then the probability that positive change will take place is increased. Overall, it is suggested that groups have to be 'homogeneous enough to ensure stability and heterogeneous enough to ensure vitality'. Such groups seem to offer greater opportunities for learning and benefiting from each other. Paradise and Daniels (1972) examine group composition in relation to its goals, appropriately adding that this is but one factor of many 'which bear heavily on a group's movement towards its goals'. The task-centred and time-limited approach adopted by most group workers in this field, even when the approach is more experiential, seems to play down leadership rivalries, task avoidance and undue dependency. Group leaders generally see themselves as providing a relaxed and easy atmosphere which generates trust and encourages sharing between members. They see that the group keeps to its task and where indicated they provide information to enable the group to carry on with its educative work.

Evaluation

Empirical evidence to support the underlying assumptions about the use of groups in preparing and assessing adoptive and foster parents is still very thin, reflecting no doubt the novelty of the approach. Crowley (1982), for example, suggests that foster parents who had attended a training course felt much better prepared for their role than those who had not. Based also on her study of new foster parents, Cautley (1980) claims that among the help and support needed by many of the families and judged to be 'a good investment' were pre-placement preparation for the commitment required and for the difficulties of foster children, early and continued post-placement support and reassurance and training in handling behaviour, especially in positive reinforcement techniques. Cautley does not distinguish though between group and individual preparation/training/support, but presumably, most of these can be more easily accomplished through groups. A study by Boyd and Remy (1979) found that trained foster parents were more likely to keep children in their care for longer periods of time and they were also more likely to continue for longer as foster parents. The authors acknowledge though, that perhaps the more capable families might have elected to participate in training and would have done a better job even if they had not received training. Simon and Simon's (1982) findings also support the view that foster parents' training increases the stability of children's placements, a point supported by some of the carers contributing to this volume. Berridge and Cleaver (1986) established, among other things, that 'the preparatory training of foster parents was found to be rewarded with greater stability'. Hampson (1985) concludes from a review of the literature that foster parent training can be effective. Macaskill (1984) comments from her study of families who adopted mentally handicapped children that families which went through individual interviews did not seem to absorb much from the experience, in spite of the wide range of topics discussed. In contrast, she adds, group meetings made a lasting impression on those who attended them.

Based on findings from their recent study, Kagan and Reid (1986) make a case for careful preparation and for post-adoptive services to adoptive families in handling the experience of grief, loss, detachment and anger that an older, emotionally disturbed youth is likely to exhibit within the adoptive family. The authors claim that the ability of the adoptive parents to handle such feelings is an indication of success in the adoptive placement of older children. Cohen's (1984) study found that poorly prepared adoptive parents felt less satisfied with the placement and Lahti (1982) claimed that the child's well-being was strongly influenced by adoptive parents' knowledge of the child's past and by preparation for the child's arrival in the home. Jarrett and Copher (1980) comment on the value of pre-placement in groups in assessing the parents' motivation and potential for adoption and for providing information on the adoption process, advice on problems to expect with children and specific information on specific children. It is further claimed that groups led by fellow adoptive parents lessen the burden of the social worker and enhance the involvement of potential adoptive parents.

The contributors to this section examine the preparation of adoptive and/or foster parents through the use of groups from the perspective of their respective agencies. Overlaps in the approach are inevitable because of the way practitioners influence each other, particularly in the 'small' world of adoption and fostering. There is, equally, distinctiveness, as between Carole Smith's more 'educative approach' and Gerry O'Hara's 'self-reflective' model. Chris Fines describes the move from predominantly information-giving sessions to a more experiential process. More fundamentally, Ottis Edwards, Cecily Griffith and Beryl Jefferies demonstrate how the group content can be adapted to reflect the circumstances and position of black and mixed couples and also respond to the needs of black children in care.

2

Groupwork with prospective foster and adoptive parents

Carole Smith

INTRODUCTION

Working with prospective foster and adoptive parents as a means of education and preparation has long been established practice in the United States. From somewhat patchy beginnings (see Parfit, 1971) this approach has become popular as a major part of fostering and adoption practice in Britain. Certainly, as Douglas points out, 'there is considerable evidence to the effect that learning which takes place within a group situation and which the group accepts as its own effort, rather than coming from without, is effective learning' (1976, p. 48). However, there is also ample evidence that for learning to occur within a group, and for it to be maintained when the group has finished, certain conditions must prevail.

Absorbing information, applying it to personal and social circumstances, testing out its validity and using it as a springboard for change, requires the kind of group which facilitates learning. Research and practice literature has identified the following properties as encouraging this result: the availability and expression of support; opportunities for exchanging and discussing advice and ideas; acceptable influence and reinforcement from peers; joint problem solving; enhancement of self-disclosure and feedback from group members; role modelling and application of feelings and behaviour to one's own situation. The group must be small enough to engage members in interaction and sufficiently large to provide resources of ideas, opinions, attitudes and problem-solving approaches – in effect, no more than fourteen participants. Additionally a group's activity must focus on a shared purpose and people must have enough in common to generate mutual support and cohesion. In his review of small group research Smith (1980) concludes that for learning to be internalised groups must *always* create trust, cohesion and a supportive climate but must *also* introduce and accommodate confrontation and conflict. Dissonant information provides the impetus for internal reassessment, struggle and change.

Groups develop and change. Tuckman (1965) identifies the stages of forming, storming, norming and performing. Forming comprises tentative contact and mutual exploration where dependence on the group leader is high. Storming represents an individual-group struggle where members may resist cohesion, assert their own status and power and challenge other participants and the leader. Norming indicates that the group has reached some cohesion and agreed to work on the task. This phase runs into performing where the group uses its own resources for problem solving. Ignorance of such processes may engender high anxiety and inappropriate leader-responses with consequent heightening of group hostility and insecurity.

The group leader must keep an instrumental-maintenance balance throughout the group's life, combining giving directions, initiating activities, summarising, clarifying, evaluating, along with reality-testing with enhancing the group's emotional climate and security through encouraging, rewarding, compromising, tension reduction and mediating in inter-personal conflicts. It may be helpful for co-leaders to split these responsibilities between them. Leaders must assess the group's development and move out of a central person role as cohesion and confidence grows. Additionally if leaders impose a high degree of structure and control throughout, they may set up a pattern of compliance and identification so that learning will prove non-transferable from the group setting (see Smith, 1980).

As social workers, it is arguable that we have sometimes been guilty of assuming that we have the necessary knowledge and skills to make groups work. Despite the brevity of the above remarks, it should be evident that effective groupwork is not a simple matter. What follows is a description of four sessions for prospective substitute parents who want to care for older children (five plus) on a long-term basis. The content was designed particularly for this purpose and exemplifies some elements of group functioning and learning.

Session one: Setting the scene

(1) **Introduction – The contract**: An explanation of overall aims of the

meetings, which are generally to help people consider some of the issues and experiences (feelings and behaviour) involved in fostering and adoption, to explore what these will mean for their families and to develop a better understanding of the tasks, challenges and rewards which lie ahead. Films, tapes and worksheets will be used to stimulate ideas and discussion. We emphasize that we will *not* be taking note of individual reactions, that we do *not* expect people to behave like amateur psychologists, and we will *not* award black marks to those who prefer to listen. We *will* have something to learn from each other and the meetings provide an opportunity to exchange, develop and generate ideas.

(2) **Introducing ourselves**: participants are asked to interview someone they don't know and to jot down (cards and pencils provided) some basic information, for example name, job, family details, interests, what they hope to get out of the group meetings. Each member then introduces the person they have interviewed to the group and explains a little about them.

(3) **Parenting and parenting plus**: first we ask participants to think about what being a parent involves and to 'brainstorm' their ideas which are recorded on a large, visible sheet of paper. When this list is exhausted we request some thoughts about the kinds of extras which might be apparent in fostering or adoption. Responses are again written up on a separate sheet. Brainstorming and recording are immediate activities and time is allowed for discussing information which the group itself has produced.

(4) **How will it affect our family?**: participants are divided into two small groups and asked to consider a worksheet which includes quotations from families, friends and neighbours of foster and adoptive parents. We request that they apply the worksheets to their own situations in terms of the reactions which they may encounter and ways of responding to those. The groups are given sheets of paper so that they can record deliberations and we ask that a spokesperson is delegated to report back when the two groups come together to discuss their ideas.

(5) **Film – Where the Love Starts**: this film has considerable emotional impact so we ask participants to remember just one thing

that particularly strikes them and we get an immediate response from each member at the end of the film.

Comment

Much has been written about the importance of the contract which will govern a group's programme, design and expectations. Because of the nature of the education and preparation groups, the contract is largely non-negotiable but it must be made clear right at the beginning. Participants are treated as adults who have a right to know what will happen. The 'introducing ourselves' activity is used to speed up interaction with the purpose of enhancing some initial feeling of communality of interest and mutual support. We use this approach because it emphasizes each individual's membership of the group and is less demanding than, for example, trust exercises at a time when leaders are trying to enhance feelings of safety and security. Even so, in one of our groups we managed to paralyse one person with anxiety because she couldn't write and thought we were going to collect up the cards and look at them – another point to remember!

'Parenting and Parenting Plus' engages the whole group in producing ideas, and 'How will it affect our family' begins more intensive small group problem-solving. Here we have very quickly moved into the group using its own resources and taking responsibility for what it produces. Some resistance may be met along the lines of refusing to consider any 'pluses' for foster or adoptive parenting or asserting that 'what we decide to do is our decision and has nothing to do with our families or friends'. If pushed, leaders can give examples but should ideally seek challenges to these attitudes from other group members. Throughout this session, leaders will be concerned to generate a sense of security and group cohesion. This must start right at the beginning with everything organized and coffee or tea at the ready. Leaders refer to the group as a whole (including themselves), thus placing authority and responsibility firmly with the group and refusing to take an all-powerful role. Response to 'Where the Love Starts' begins to get at common feelings which leaders will acknowledge as being inherently valid.

Session two: Being in care

(1) **Introduction**: Leaders summarize the last session and explain the aims of this session. Questions are invited before moving on; these are not necessarily answered in a direct way but may be referred back to the group.

(2) **Reasons for coming into care**: participants are asked to brainstorm why they think children come into care and to rank order the reasons in terms of frequency. Comments are recorded as previously explained. We then pin up statistical information and compare results.

(3) **Separation and loss**: we are lucky here to have a very good tape recording made by a young adult whom I shall call Joan. After numerous admissions to care she and her slightly younger half-brother were placed in a Children's Home following the death of their mother. They remained in residential care until Joan, at 13, and her half-brother, went to live with foster parents. On this part of the tape Joan refers to how little she remembers of her early life and how she has no recollection of her mother.

(4) **Being received into care**: participants again move into two small groups and consider a work sheet recording children's comments about how they felt when they were admitted to care. One group is asked to consider how these quotations make them feel and the other to discuss how the children feel. Each group is given a sheet of paper and a spokesperson is asked to report back to the full group.

(5) **Falling apart**: Joan talks on tape about how she felt when told, at 13, that her brother had a different biological father. She recalls her reactions vividly, saying that she felt as though she had lost part of herself, that she was nothing and that she had failed. She then goes on to discuss the lack of continuity which she experienced while in care with workers coming and going around her.

(6) **How would you feel?**: we ask participants to close their eyes for a few minutes and to remember an experience of loss, separation or a new and daunting situation. Leaders do the same. They then brainstorm how they are feeling. There is usually little hesitation in producing a list which includes anger, confusion, despair, loneliness, anxiety, pain and

so on. The group is encouraged to relate these feelings to the responses of children entering care, their behaviour and appropriate reactions and management by foster and adoptive parents.

OR: the group is given an imaginary exercise involving separation and asked to verbally explore their responses. An activity such as 'sculpting' helps to reflect how members experience separation and loss if the climate is assessed by leaders as being sufficiently secure and if group support is high.

(7) **Living in a children's home**: Joan talks about her experience of residential care. She refers to well-intentioned visitors, inflexible routine, lack of privacy and feeling like a spare part who has to fit into organizational and bureaucratic priorities.

Comment

Leaders begin to move out of a central person role, encouraging group cohesion by referring problems back and using verbal signals such as 'we', 'the group', 'our experience' and so on. The 'reasons for coming into care' exercise starts reality testing and challenges popular myths about the number of orphans in care, incidents of abuse/neglect and the ages of children for whom family placements might be sought. Small groups enable members to explore feelings safely while coming together in the full group maintains cohesion. The 'how would you feel' activity is emotionally laden and leaders must be alert to group maintenance functions. 'Living in a children's home' is purposely introduced at the end of this session to give the groups something more tangible to discuss. Members need an opportunity to pull out of the introspection of dealing with their own feelings and they can safely direct their anger about what we have done to them at the disadvantages of residential care.

Session three: The child's background and family

(1) **Introduction** and invitation to raise questions as before.

(2) **Feelings about natural parents**: participants are divided into three small groups. They are given a work sheet with a number of quotations from foster and adoptive parents about the attitudes and behaviour of natural parents which have led to tensions and difficulties in placement.

Each group has a particular task. The first considers the material from a foster/adoptive parent's point of view, the second from the child's position and the third from the stance of natural parents. When the groups come together they are encouraged to develop a dialogue between them, arguing and exploring each case in a threesome of natural parent, substitute parent and child.

(3) **Empty chair**: the full group is asked to imagine that a natural parent is sitting in this chair and to brainstorm questions, feelings or indeed anything which they want to say. Comments are written up on a large visible sheet of paper.

(4) **Film: 'Don't Condemn Me 'til you Know Me'**: this is an emotive and explanatory film which features natural parents talking about having their children in care and their attitudes towards foster and adoptive parents. Afterwards participants compare the film with their brainstormed responses to the empty chair and consider how their reactions might be modified by what natural parents have actually expressed.

(5) **Handling the child's background**: participants think about ways in which they understand and know about their past. These ideas are brainstormed and the group is encouraged to relate these taken-for-granted sources of information and confirmation to the experience of children in care. Members inevitably begin to explore how they can help children understand and manage the past as a positive exercise, rather than denying what has happened or resisting the intrusion of memories and significant others into their families.

(6) **Confidentiality**: a list of categorical statements is pinned up including such remarks as, 'I would never breach a confidence', 'I would breach a confidence if I thought it was in the best interests of the person who had made it', and so on. Group members are asked to indicate, without discussion, which of the statements they agree with.

(7) **Confidentiality – problem solving**: participants move into two small groups and are given a sheet recording four situations in which confidentiality is an issue. They are asked to decide what they would do as foster or adoptive parents. Paper is provided for them to record their

33

decisions and a member is nominated by each group to report back. The two groups can test out their conclusions against each other, finding confirmation or having to negotiate a challenge to intended management of the problem.

Comment

The 'feelings about natural parents' exercise is designed to generate a role-play situation between three small groups. Leaders can facilitate this by generating confrontation. Sometimes a member will refuse to join in, saying for example, 'I can't pretend to be a natural parent – my child would never end up in care.' Leaders can appeal to a challenge from the other 'natural parents' asking, 'how do you other natural parents feel about that?' In other words, 'this is a slur on you – this member is suggesting that you are so bad or different that she can't identify with you!' Participants are given permission to be absolutely free in making comments to the empty chair with the result that some pretty angry remarks may be made. We were so successful in reducing compliance in our last group that one member, already involved in a difficult fostering situation, told the imaginery parent to 'piss off'. When members have seen the film they usually feel deflated and despondent about the strength and negative contents of their brain-storming. Leaders can alleviate these feelings by encouraging the group to consider more constructive responses to natural parents. The group thus takes back responsibility for re-thinking its attitude and is motivated to make amends. Maintenance functions are important. If the group is allowed to feel too depressed it will not respond to the challenge of coping with dissonant tensions between its own reactions to the empty chair and information from the film.

'Handling the child's background' allows the group to consolidate a constructive approach to handling physically present natural parents or information about a child's past. It is sometimes surprising to see what clicks with particular members. We once had a participant who stubbornly refused to acknowledge any of the 'pluses' which the group had been discussing. At this point, however, he suddenly recognized the difference between his own history of memories, photographs, family gatherings etc., and the distorted or attenuated biography of a child in care. He said something like 'My God, it must be awful – all those things that I've taken for granted and these kids haven't got any of them!' His reward for this breakthrough came from within the group, as members had been struggling with his intransigence for some time and he had been in danger of taking on a scapegoat role. Exercises regarding confidentiality include reality-testing (it isn't as simple as it appears at first glance!), and small group problem-solving.

Session four: Living with a family

(1) **Introduction** and invitation to raise questions as before.

(2) **Moving in**: Joan talks on tape about her fears and hopes for the future and the difficulties of moving into a new family.

(3) **The family's reaction**: participants move into two small groups. One is asked to consider how they can help a child settle in to their family and the other is asked to think about what they take for granted about family life. Paper is again provided and a spokesperson is requested to report back on behalf of each group. With appropriate leadership help the two groups come together and begin to explore how ideas about helping a child will confront, and demand changes, in what they take for granted about family life.

(4) **Learning confidence**: here Joan talks about how she gradually learned to cope with living in a family and developed confidence in a number of areas. She graphically describes, however, her continuing fear of being rejected and sent back to the children's home.

(5) **Vignettes**: Leaders describe a number of difficult situations involving the behaviour of foster/adopted children. Half way through they stop and ask the group, 'What would you do?' Responses are written up on a visible sheet of paper and then the stories are completed by reading out how foster or adoptive parents actually responded.

(6) **Living with two people**: Joan describes the strains and peculiarities of living in a family – being frightened to approach her foster mother when she was ill, accommodating emotional closeness, coping with attention and inevitable demands, accepting boundaries and so on. The group is able to link her comments with the taken-for-granted expectations and experiences of family life which it has already identified.

(7) **Placement creates new relationships**: here we use a 'Parenting Plus' cartoon to demonstrate that when a child is placed there is a change in the balance of existing relationships, patterns of interaction and networks of communication within the new family. The cartoon shows a husband and wife having a row about their foster child who is listening through a keyhole. The child has apparently stolen a watch and lied about it into the bargain. Two small groups consider the cartoon and one decides how they would handle the situation while the other examines the behaviour, feelings and reactions of the child. When the groups come together they are encouraged to enter into direct discussion from their particular vantage points. The child's group may become angry about the assumption of stealing; the foster parents group may try reasonable negotiation and be met with resentment and defiance; the situation may develop nicely with someone from the child's group yelling 'I don't care what you think, I'm going to pack my bags,' or 'You can't talk to me like that – I hate you – I'm going to call my social worker.'

   OR: the cartoon may be role-played, followed by a discussion about how the participants felt and the best way of making progress with the problem.

(8) **Parenting needs**: Joan tries to explain why her family placement disrupted and clearly identifies her inability to meet the needs of her foster parents. It is apparent that Joan accepted responsibility for 'failure' and that her foster parents, because of their own expectations, were unable to function as adults and to shoulder their own responsibilities as parents.

(9) **Challenges and rewards**: the group takes an overview of the four sessions, pulling out the challenges and rewards with the help of an experienced foster or adoptive parent.

(10) **Questions and explanation of what happens next**

Comment

By now leaders will have withdrawn from the role of central person, intervening only to explain tasks or to facilitate, encourage, expand or mediate in interpersonal (or inter-group) conflicts if people get stuck.

The group is helped in problem-solving by clues which are provided on Joan's tape. Vignettes and the 'Parenting Plus' cartoon focus attention on particular behaviour and situations and invite participants to anticipate and practise problem-solving responses. If the cartoon promotes angry inter-group confrontation, leaders may have to provide a way out by interjecting in the role of foster parents, 'I think we are just making each other madder – let's calm down and leave things until tomorrow'; or providing reassurance that social workers are accustomed to being used as weapons by upset children; or encouraging clarification by suggesting that the conflicting factions should backtrack and try to work out how they got themselves into such a mess. Leadership intervention has changed from facilitating interaction and group cohesion to signalling alternatives to the group and allowing avenues of escape if challenge and confrontation threaten the group's maintenance needs.

SOME GENERAL OBSERVATIONS

Several general comments should be added to those following each of the sessions. Although the programme is highly structured in terms of content, leaders avoid taking on an authority role or the exercise and attribution of power. We always leave the room when small groups are operating in order to reduce dependence, encourage member initiatives and make it clear that responsibility for problem-solving lies with the group. Leader interventions are designed to enhance the group's independence once the initial phase of 'forming' shows signs of moving towards mutual support and cohesion. During these interludes we often make pots of coffee and tea and deliver them to the group. Although a small point, participants then have to organize the refreshments and this gets people moving about and increases member interaction.

Throughout the programme there are opportunities to choose between safer alternatives, like group discussion, and role play or other activities. Talking about the groups run by Parents for Children, Juliet Horne suggests that 'role play was too threatening and too intrusive to use with applicants' (1983, p. 13). We think, however, that if leaders have accurately assessed the group climate and sense of security then role play, sculpting or other exercises may be used to beneficial effect. Using groups to achieve learning means that the group's own resources must be employed to this end. Leaders must be alert to factors which may interfere with this, including the existence of 'monopolizers', (people who talk too much and make a play for leadership), and those who frustrate the group by withdrawing co-operation or involvement. Various ploys may be introduced to ameliorate these problems by, for example, suggesting that someone different is chosen to report back from small groups, asking the group if there is a different angle to the problem, suggesting that sometimes people find groups difficult and so on. A combination of small groups and the whole group encourages everyone to participate in whichever milieu is most comfortable and attempts to achieve a balance between cohesion and confrontation. The group is encouraged to make links between the material from different sessions thus emphasizing the validity of recurring themes. Joan's tape provides continuity over the four sessions and generates an identification with her perceptions and experiences.

Clearly, an important development in group work is to make such education and preparation both accessible and acceptable to Afro-Caribbean and Asian families. We have, with careful preliminary thought and detailed explanation, included such applicants in our groups but have never had sufficient numbers at the right time to arrange groups with a total membership of ethnic minority families. The logistics of doing so are enormous. However, we must consider the dangers of running groups on the basis of a multitude of factors which we take for granted but which we know may be alien to Afro-Caribbean and Asian families. The literature is now replete with reminders that social workers must suspend some of their normal values and expectations when working with ethnic minority applicants (see Small 1982; Brunton and Welch, 1983; Schroeder et al, 1985). When including such applicants in our groups, leaders have so far been able to maintain mutual support and cohesion while the Afro-Caribbean and Asian members have introduced useful challenges regarding attitudes and child-rearing practices.

SUMMARY

We are now well past the time when education and preparation groups were regarded as a novelty. The introduction of 'Parenting Plus' and 'Added to Adolescence' galvanized many agencies into action when they enthusiastically took up the offer of a ready designed programme and training for group leaders. Since then some agencies have creatively expanded and developed work in small groups to cover a whole range of fostering schemes and educational needs (see for example Barker and Hutchings, 1981; Bastian and Odams, 1983; Davis et al, 1984). We know that using the resources of small groups can bring about learning and change, but only if we heed the theory and research which is available: there is a world of difference between a collection of people having a conversation and a small group which generates learning through its own endeavours.

3

Preparing families in groups
Gerry O'Hara

The Agency

Lothian Region's child care policy was re-organized in the early 1980s into either time-limited task-oriented fostering or permanent parenting. In permanent placements, whether adoption or fostering, the intention was that families 'assume a full parental role' (McKay, 1980). The Social Work Department also adopted a policy that it should work to an explicit target where no child under 12 should remain in care for more than two years, and that if rehabilitation to their natural family was not possible then the child should be resettled in a permanent substitute family within that time span. It was the intention that unless otherwise indicated the permanent home should be an adoptive one, at least for children under ten.

Among other resources for children's services a specialist homefinding team was established by directly transferring funds from the closure of children's homes. There was then a clear commitment to close a number of children's homes and transfer resources to develop a range of community services for children. The Homefinding Team was established with the remit to place the children who had been in care for some time as well as those who were continuing to be referred for permanent placement. Broadly speaking the aims and objectives of the Homefinding Team were to recruit, prepare and assess families offering permanent new homes to special needs children and to support such placements. Specifically there was a commitment to:
(1) Radically alter our preparation/assessment process to make it more meaningful and relevant to families.
(2) Develop recruitment strategies that avoided children being involved in direct media publicity whilst placing them as quickly as possible.

40

(3) Develop a post-placement support service that would be used by both adopters and foster parents who had taken children on a permanent basis.

In this chapter an attempt is made to describe the development of our preparation groupwork with prospective adoptive parents and with foster parents who apply to take children on a permanent basis.

WHAT WE ARE PREPARING FAMILIES FOR

The dilemma for those of us working with prospective adopters or foster parents who wish to make a permanent commitment to a child in care is how we find out with them what their needs and expectations are, and what they really feel and understand about the children available for placement, and the often intractable problems they will bring with them to the new family. We are asking for families who want to make a permanent commitment to a special needs child, to have respect for what the child is now, to value him enough to allow his individuality to impact on and make changes in the rest of the family, and to welcome the new influence as a means for all of them to learn and grow together. We realize that this is a tall order. Most applicants if faced with this challenge might agree with these ideas, but in reality would not be able to understand its enormity without a lot of help from the agency, tremendously hard work on their part, and ultimately the reality of living with the child on a day to day basis. Part, therefore, of the preparation/assessment process is seen as being the acceptance by both the family and the agency worker of their shared responsibility for finding out together how the prospective family really operates, what their strengths and areas of vulnerability are, including the quality of nurturing and stimulation, sources available for support and understanding their values and outlook, and how they have evolved over time. For example, are their values seen as immutable truths or do they change and develop with new experiences? They need to somehow learn, with the agency's help, that their family is an operational 'system' which will be very much changed by what they are planning. Part of the objective of the assessment and preparation process is to help them to see this.

The agency will not only be working with families in preparation for the placement of a special needs child, but will be setting the tone for ongoing post-placement support work. Experience suggests that such support is necessary, even if only from time to time until perhaps the

41

vicissitudes of childhood are over. The children we place cannot just be slotted into new families and left there without follow-up. As a former colleague put it, 'there may be a lot of trials, tribulations, testing and general traumas on all sides, but when all that is finally over the child should know that he is wanted and loved and will be able to become a fully fledged member of his new family'.

The danger is, of course, that the child who is not 'grateful' and does not slot into his allotted place may be rejected. Families who start out with this approach need to be challenged and have their expectations questioned. Workers approaching permanent family placement with the 'slotting in' theory will need to re-examine what it is families can be expected to give these damaged children. How we facilitate the shared responsibility and task of preparation and assessment is determined largely by our acceptance and understanding of special needs adoption and fostering, their possibilities and limitations. We need to resist the approach which implicitly seeks solutions and happy endings. What is required is a realistic and gritty approach to the challenge which will inform more relevant preparation and ongoing support for these placements. We respond to these challenges by acknowledging the agency's responsibility and its authority to ultimately accept or reject any application. As a result we have broken down our assessment/ preparation process into three distinct stages:

1. the initial recruitment and giving of information about children who need families;
2. the preparation, training and self-assessment; and
3. the home study and final decision-making.

STAGE 1: THE INITIAL RECRUITMENT AND GIVING OF INFORMATION

Broadly speaking this stage involves identifying prospective substitute families in the community by giving information about our need through the media (we do not seek media exposure of children waiting). Thereafter, we encourage families to come along to one of our open information evenings. Families who continue to be interested are then given one or two preliminary interviews, with the emphasis on information about the children who are waiting and the adoption process itself. At this stage, we do not expect families to give us any information but rather we see our task as explaining very broadly why children come into care, why some of them will never be able to return home, and beginning the attempt to identify some of the problems that children who have experienced separation from their own families will bring to new placements. If, after this initial stage, there is a wish to proceed, the families are invited to a series of six preparation groups. It is only after the preparation groups that families are encouraged to formally apply if they have decided at that stage that this is what they wish to do.

STAGE 2: PREPARATION AND SELF-ASSESSMENT

In common with many other agencies throughout the country we have developed a groupwork approach to the preparation of families interested in permanent substitute family care. Groupwork programmes for the preparation of families interested in adopting or fostering special needs children were pioneered in the UK by such agencies as Parents for Children and Barnardo's New Families Project (Glasgow) from the mid-1970s onwards. Both of these agencies were largely influenced by the approach of the American agency 'Spalding for Children' which had been involved in a lot of exciting and encouraging work. Underpinning this approach, which attempted to separate out preparation for the task in groups from the formal home study, was the work of people such as the Kirks (1964 and 1970).

The Kirks were honest, realistic and also visionary. However, even if we provide what they describe as 'educational opportunities' for families considering the placement of special needs children, to give them the opportunity to decide if they want to go ahead and apply, we have to acknowledge that there will still be many obstacles to realistic parent preparation. The following barriers to learning have emerged from our work experience:

A preoccupation with being accepted; a reluctance or resistance to learn or be reflective about parenting; a resistance to working in groups, or learning from social workers, particularly if the latter are childless.

There are many other personal barriers to learning which prospective carers may bring, the ultimate one being the lack of reality of the actual experience. All these possible barriers have to be recognized and worked with. In structuring our groups we have drawn considerably on the understanding of how adults learn, and on our knowledge about small groups. We also work with the knowledge that peer groups are only part of a home-study process. The preparation work and information giving go on throughout the pre-placement phase.

Aims and objectives of a groupwork approach to substitute carers

The ultimate aim of parent preparation is to identify and prepare parents for the successful permanent placement of special needs children. It is essential for the success of this approach that prospective adopters are treated as responsible individuals who have the ability to decide, with guidance, whether special needs adoption is appropriate for them. As an agency we recognize that adoptive parents have some needs of their own, but more important that they are valuable resources. The real clients in this situation are the children. Within this atmosphere the following objectives are pursued:

A. *Self-assessment*
  - to provide those interested in adoption and fostering with enough information to determine whether the process with the agency is an option they want to consider;
  - to provide prospective parents with the type of structure that enables them to begin assessing for themselves their notional capability and commitment to parenting a special needs child;
  - to provide a process that enables prospective parents to participate in determining the type of child or the specific child they want to parent;
  - to provide encouragement and support to help parents strengthen their commitment to successfully parenting a special needs child.

B. *Preparation objectives*
  - to provide prospective parents with a basic framework for understanding parent/child interactions;
  - to explore the process by which we build significant relationships with others (both adults and children);
  - to explore with parents the process by which they acquire values and transmit them to their children;
  - to assist families in acceptance of both positive and negative feelings in themselves and others;
  - to help prospective parents develop parenting techniques that may be particularly appropriate in parenting special needs children;

- to help each family assess the kinds of support they already have and develop others they may need;
- to provide families with opportunities to develop empathy for the child they are going to parent;
- to strengthen the network through prospective parents assisting and supporting one another before and after the placement.

CONTENT

This model provides for a series of seven sessions, each lasting approximately two hours, usually in the evenings in our homefinding meeting room. The group optimally consists of two social workers co-leading the group, one or two couples who are experienced carers and three to five prospective new families. The material becomes increasingly experiential over the seven sessions. Prospective parents have the opportunity to test out their attitudes, values and experiences through discussion and a variety of group activities. A range of other opportunities are provided to help them evaluate their own strengths, limitations, flexibility and reservations. The process places them in a better position to decide and also prepares them for the task of parenting a special needs child.

The following is a very brief précis of the six sessions:

Pre-group orientation – An overview of the adoption process with questions and answers. (Described earlier as an information meeting).

Session one – Panel discussion: Adoptive families talk about their own experiences.

Session two – Preparation for parenting the challenging child: Understanding self and others as a base for successful placement.

Session three – How we make relationships: Looking at how our relationships can be improved, especially with adopted children.

Session four – When children come into care: Learning to accept and cope with a child's past.

Session five – Styles of parenting: Looking at how we were parented and how we choose to parent our own children.

Session six – Where do we get help to make placements work? and Where do we go from here?

Structure and leadership

Clarity about the role of the leadership, and the composition, size, and nature of the group are just as important as understanding its purpose, methods and principles. For example, the leadership has to be open from the beginning about the extent of its authority and power, particularly with regard to the outcome of the group members' applications – in other words, to acknowledge its evaluative role. Cartwright (1967) stresses the importance of acknowledging this authority at the outset, despite changes liable to occur in progress. We have found that whether or not we are explicit, families are quite clear of the leadership's substantial power to influence the outcome of their application. This somewhat contradicts Kirk's ideas (1964 and 1970), and it is not surprising that such groups do become preoccupied with approval.

Lieberman et al. (1973) suggests that there are four dimensions of effective leader behaviour: (1) Executive function, which is defined in terms of behaviour such as limit setting, suggesting or setting rules, limits, norms, setting goals or directions of movement, managing time, sequencing, pacing, blocking, stopping, interceding and so on; (2) Caring, which is defined as a leader style which involves protecting, offering friendship, love, affection and frequent invitations for members to seek feedback as well as support, praise and encouragement; (3) Emotional stimulation, which represents leader behaviour stressing the revealing of feelings, challenging, confrontation, revelation of personal values, attitudes, beliefs, frequent participation as a member in a group, exhortation and drawing attention to self; (4) Meaning attribution, which involves cognitizing behaviour – that is providing concepts of how to understand, explain, clarify and interpret, and provide frameworks of change. Smith (1980) suggests that both support and confrontation are required if group learning is to be internalized and hence retained.

In order to take account of the many barriers to learning described earlier, and to increase the opportunities for group members to have the maximum opportunity to hear about family placements, both in theory and in practice, we use two social workers and two sets of experienced carers to both lead and resource the group. Broadly speaking, the two social workers are expected to fulfil and share equally the leadership dimensions already mentioned, and the experienced carers are able to bring the reality of family placement to assist the learning and preparation of the prospective adoptive or foster parents. We have found that some people learn very little from social workers and much more from experienced carers and other group members. Others seem to learn from a combination of social workers and/or adopters and group members. We try to maximize the learning opportunities for the members by using their own experiences, that of the carers and the knowledge of social workers. We demonstrate our valuing of the skills of the experienced carers by paying them for their involvement in these groups, as well as providing them with support and consultation.

In line with Bertcher and Maple (1977), we plan group composition and try to mix the group to include both childless couples and those with their own children. Similarly, we try to ensure, not always easy, a mix of social and educational backgrounds. Most applicants seem able to function in the group, but a great number also drop out before they start, and it is hard to know whether they do so because of the prospect of the groups.

Theoretical background

The major theoretical influences underpinning this direction in parent preparation, which grows out of an ecological systems perspective, are described by Hartman (1979). She defines the assessment process as a shared responsibility between social worker and family. As far as possible the worker's role is to help members of the family gain more information and understanding about their family and wider environment, and to give them as much information as possible about adoption and fostering in general and of particular children to be considered. On the basis of an enhanced understanding of the family and knowledge about the demands of the task, the worker helps the family to make a decision about adoption or fostering and, if they decide to adopt or foster, helps them prepare.

Hartman goes on to describe in great detail a model that links preparation, parenting training and self-assessment in groups, with an individual worker and family home study. Our model has also been influenced by Satir's work (1967 and 1970), and by Morrison (1980), whose writings, ideas and influences in the transactional analysis field we draw upon.

Brief summary of sessions

Session 1: The purpose of this session is to help prospective families to further explore whether they wish to pursue special needs adoption or fostering. The session is relatively structured in order to introduce the group to the reality of family placement right from the outset, without placing too much pressure on applicants to speak or reveal much, if anything of themselves. As a result no formal introductions are made but name tags are handed out. Only the group leaders and the experienced carers introduce themselves. The stress of formal group introduction should not be underestimated. The session consists of two parts – firstly, the two experienced carers discuss their reasons for adopting or fostering the type of child they decided on and their own preparation experiences. They normally share their families' and friends' reactions, initial problems which occurred, and their feelings around the time they met their children. The second part of the session is devoted to the period following placement, the adjustments they and the children had to make and how they helped the children to do this. They discuss particular behaviours and their handling and the effects of these on other children in the family. Other topics covered include conflicts over differing values, school problems and discipline. Throughout the session, applicants are free to ask questions, although normally the social workers take the experienced carers through these areas. Typically at this stage, applicants are keen to find out more about the preparation and assessment procedure because they are currently experiencing the process. Carers who are able to share experiences with honesty and a touch of humour, and who are not afraid to put into words their own preoccupations and concerns, are usually experienced as helpful and reassuring.

Session 2: The first part of this session is meant to provide prospective families with the opportunity to continue self-assessment through an exercise. The second part aims to promote reflection on the parent/ child relationship and provide some insight into how to increase self-esteem in children. There is pressure on applicants, mostly couples, to participate in reflecting on their values and their own experiences as children and/or parents through:

(i)   Group sharing – a brief introduction and direct questioning of group members about which child or type of child they would like to adopt and why.
(ii) An individual activity – a fun exercise designed to help families describe what they like to do best.
(iii) A brief presentation and worksheet – to promote understanding of parent/child relationships.
(iv) An exercise demonstrating the confusing values children in care can be subjected to.

For example, the individual activity designed to encourage applicants to share what they like to do best is a simple questionnaire asking them to describe, in brainstorming fashion, the 20 things they like doing best. Simple things, like reading the papers or going for a walk, are the kinds of activities that frequently rank in the 'Top 20', and much humour about the things people like to do best usually abounds in this session. Applicants are then encouraged to share their answers and, not surprisingly, the favourite 20 activities are very different from person to person. An important point made during this session is that some things will have to go, whilst other activities will have to be broadened to include the children. Experienced foster and adoptive parents usually make useful contributions about the kind of things they had to give up in order to parent their adopted or fostered child.

Another activity in this session is a brief presentation followed by a worksheet exercise designed to begin to encourage applicants to reflect on the way they themselves were parented and how this has affected their values, attitudes and communication patterns. The particular worksheet we use, and this can be adapted, involves a series of probing questions, such as:

What messages did your parents give you about the following?
(Members are expected to write their answers after each sentence.)

1. Doing work.
2. Using money.
3. Being a man or woman.
4. Achieving success.
5. Being good or bad.

6. Enjoying your body, etc.

The answers are less important than the opportunity for discussing values and how these evolved. The exercise encourages the notion that the way applicants were parented will affect their parental attitudes and expectations. It is not unusual for group members sometimes to challenge a social worker's statement, with other members joining in. For example, the worker's comment that 'our childhood influences directly affect the way we bring up our own children or children who might be placed with us' started a long discussion on discipline and what children should be allowed to do or say.

From this developing self-awareness it is somewhat easier to help group members to understand how much more confusing the acquisition of values and communication patterns can be for a child joining their family who has previously had inconsistent parenting. We take the simple approach of asking two group members in turn to read out a series of contradictory, value-laden statements which may have been given to separated children, e.g. 'always flush the toilet at night', followed by 'don't flush the toilet at night, you'll waken people up.' The exercise continues in this vein towards more complicated messages which children will have received, e.g. 'always be nice to people, hide your feelings because you don't want people to be upset.' This contrasts with 'always say what you think and be honest with people.' Building on the earlier examination of their own experiences as children in families, this exercise helps them understand that if their own family communication patterns were complicated, it is much more so for separated children. The session finishes with a very brief presentation to encourage a discussion about how group members express anger, linked with the anger that children in care may feel.

Session 3: This session builds on the previous one and looks at how to establish positive relationships with a new family member. Among other things, emphasis is placed on how touch and time can be used to promote intimate relationships with adopted or fostered children. The session further explores values as well as biases and stereotypes, and how these influence our attitudes and behaviour towards ourselves, our family and our children. Ways of promoting these aims include:

(i)   Building on the exercise from the previous session, where applicants were asked to say what they like doing best, they are now asked to say what will need to change when a child is placed with them.

(ii) A worksheet called 'Making Choices' is distributed to group members to encourage values' clarification.

(iii) A brief presentation on how we use touch and time to both seek and avoid intimacy.

(iv) Presentation by a family who have adopted or fostered a child with a mental handicap.

The importance of helping prospective applicants look at how they use time and touch to either seek or avoid intimacy, is crucial when one thinks about the need to build meaningful relationships from a process of social engineering. For the discussion on touch, we ask people to confer in pairs or with their partners about the norms on touching that prevailed in their family when they were children; also how these have affected them. From this discussion, which typically has group members revealing that they were either always cuddled throughout their childhood, or that it stopped at a certain age or stage, e.g. when they got to adolescence, or frequently much earlier, we underline through the carers the need some older or special needs children will have for this kind of intimacy. A long discussion usually follows on cuddling and kissing with experienced carers present sharing their experience with placed children. Experienced carers present are crucial in 'punching home' the need for finding ways to make intimacy safe for both the child and the parent, and the need to set about this in a self-conscious way.

The meeting concludes with a presentation and written information about mental handicap, so that families, whether or not they are interested in a child with a handicap, can have some understanding about retardation.

Session 4: This session focusses on the dynamics of acceptance. It is designed to help prospective adoptive and foster parents apply the concepts of acceptance to their own feelings, their extended families' feelings, their adopted or fostered children's background, the children already in their home and the adopted child. This is done through:

- members sharing the attitudes of their parents, relatives and close friends to their adopting or fostering a special needs child;
- information by the leadership on why children come into care and the varied and complicated backgrounds that the caretaking families will need to begin to understand and accept as part of the child's past. When exploring this theme, one experienced carer

remarked how difficult she found it to understand or sympathize with the child's mother, because she suspected the mother used to batter the child regularly. One member's response was 'but every parent feels like this at some point.' First carer: 'Yes, but it is easier to say that than to feel it. When you get attached to these children you want to blot out all that's happened to them . . .'
 — activity designed to encourage prospective parents to check their own levels of acceptance and expectations of children who may be placed with them.

By now the sessions are into a pattern of brief presentation, much discussion and the use of worksheets to promote interaction. To check out the level of behaviour which might, or might not be acceptable to applicants, a simple worksheet which lists behaviour problems is completed by participants. The answers are in terms of what they might find acceptable, moderately unacceptable and very unacceptable. These views are then discussed to identify agreements and disagreements, and promote argument and confrontation among the group members about the level of behaviour which would be acceptable to them or not. A further worksheet is distributed asking for 'definitions' to promote discussion of levels of acceptance, expectations and values. For example, there are a series of incomplete statements which participants are asked to complete, such as:

(i)   'Love' is . . .
(ii)   To be a good parent means . . .
(iii) A good parent/child relationship means . . .
(iv)   To be comfortable with yourself means . . .
(v)   A mother should be expected to . . .
(vi)   A father should be expected to . . .
(vii) Discipline means . . .

Session 5: This session moves on to examine how families express and teach values to adopted or fostered children. The specific focus of the session is on parenting skills which clarify and consistently communicate values to children. This is done through:
A group question, for example: 'What is one of the things you value most, and do you think your new child will come into your family sharing that same value?' (At one of the sessions one of the experienced adopters commented on how when they first had Jane they used to be always on at her and would nag her about such things as her table

manners, the way she talked and looked, 'we felt as if we never gave her any rest, yet there were so many things that we wanted to change.');
A *series of probing questions* about values taken from Simon (1972) are used, but the emphasis here is on communicating values and acceptable limits of behaviour to children. A useful way of taking discussion forward after the values' clarification exercises, is for experienced carers to make brief presentations of particular issues or aspects of behaviour which they held important and attempted to communicate to their adopted child. An example might be a child who consistently lied or was abusive to adults at school or within the home. The key points for clarification are:

- the feelings of the carers about this behaviour, based on their own ideas of what is acceptable;
- how they tackled the behaviour and communicated their dis-approval of the behaviour, but acceptance of the child, to him or her;
- the importance of recognizing that it may be a very long time before change is effected;
- deciding what has to change, what might change at some time and what cannot change;
- how to demonstrate value to the child as he is, despite his/her behaviour.

Session 6: The final session continues to look at parenting skills and explores available support systems to prospective carers. Time is also set aside to answer questions not already covered, and map out the way forward. Methods used include:

(i)   an exercise highlighting the need to give positive messages to children to promote good self-image;
(ii) a presentation of the different levels of love parents may feel for their adopted or fostered children;
(iii) an exercise and worksheet designed to encourage families to identify more fully their expectations and needs at this time;
(iv) a presentation by members of the Lothian Adopters Group about the range of supports available and the need to see them as normal and necessary.

Examples of content: Group members are given the task of making positive comments about others in the group. Individuals are paired up and asked to think of two or three compliments to give the other based on their observations during the group. Depending on the participants' level of comfort in giving or receiving compliments, discussion focusses on both the advantages and the problems of building children's self-image in this way.

Through the use of 'Eco Maps' (see Hartman, 1979), families are also encouraged to look at the supports which they currently have or expect to have in coping with their adopted or fostered child. The 'Eco Map' (based on systems theory) is a commonly used tool now in assessment work. It can be demonstrated to the group by either the social worker or by one of the carers. Group members are then encouraged to complete their own 'Eco Map' with their partner and share it with others.

The experience of the carers in the group is usually complemented by a visit to the group by the Lothian Adopters' Group members who discuss the range of supports available.

Following a round-up of issues arising from a 'Way Ahead' discussion, families are given an exercise to complete at home for their home study worker to identify their expectations and needs at this time. The group material is summarized and a request made to participants to complete and return the evaluation form asking for their appraisal of the group material and experience.

Note: Though the presentation here has covered both prospective adoptive and foster parents, it is recognized that there is also a range of different tasks and expectations laid on foster carers which are tackled in separate training groups. In spite of many overlaps between adoption and foster care, there are also distinct differences between them which have to be highlighted to avoid role confusion and role distortion.

Consumer evaluation and links with home study stage

This model is relatively light on information-giving but rather concentrates on helping families be more aware of their own values, beliefs, expectations and motivation for the task. Hartman (1979) suggests that 'straight informational meetings are probably less productive than no meeting at all'. Our experience confirms this and we have found the giving and receiving of information most helpfully happens probably later in the home study stage, but most relevantly after acceptance and in the early stages of placement. Throughout the sessions we encourage sharing and learning through the use of numerous worksheets, as described. The worksheets are normally shared with the home study worker after the group, so that links between the groupwork process and the home study are forged mainly by what the family write themselves. We have found that families obviously vary in their ability to use worksheets or other written material, but this seems relatively unimportant. The important issue is that the worksheets, which ask very simple direct questions, can be used both in the groups and in the home study so that together family and worker can begin to understand the basis from which they are preparing to take on a new child.

It has been suggested that there are many families who cannot use what have been described as sophisticated learning methods and models, and that by implication we are liable to lose many otherwise good adoptive or foster parents. Although one can never know for sure, our experience and view would be that this is a somewhat patronizing attitude. Groupwork preparation should never be academic, but rather provide learning opportunities that draw on particular experiences of having lived in families. Prospective carers bring much to the learning situation and one does not need to be well-educated, or highly academic, to be able to benefit from this form of adult learning.

When we first decided to work in this way, we agreed that there should be no written information passed by the group leaders to the home study worker, and this was explained to the families. In other words, the only link between the group and the home study worker would be the worksheets which families had completed during the group and then passed on to their home study social worker. However, we found that informal 'off the record' comments were being mentioned by workers and decided that it would be more honest to complete a brief profile on each family attending the groups, share it with the families and pass it on. This can be especially important when it seems in the group that families' expectations of special needs adoption and fostering are significantly at odds with what we know to be the realities of placement. In such cases the group may not be the place to challenge these assumptions other than usually through discussion and persuasion, but in the privacy of the applicant's own home much more confronting work can be done and perhaps more efficiently so.

Very few families indeed drop out at the end of these groups. Rather, most families drop out before the groups start. This may be a reluctance to enter the process, or perhaps they realize from the outset that adoption or fostering of special needs children is a demanding and challenging task requiring more careful consideration.

SUMMARY

Workers who have been involved in running the groups compare them very favourably with our previous model which combined discussion with more information-giving and teaching, and less self-reflection than the model described here. Workers have also found these groups personally and professionally demanding. In theory it sounds good to have adoptive or foster parents as co-leaders and as colleagues in running groups, but in practice it is much more challenging. Workers need to spend time preparing, encouraging and supporting co-leaders, and trusting them to be able to deliver the goods. This model minimizes the role of the social worker as expert, and encourages the idea that almost everybody has skills in relation to parenting children which can be adjusted, altered and developed to cope with special needs placements. In order to facilitate self-reflection with group participants, leaders need to be open to it themselves. This approach should establish a tone of mutual responsibility for decision-making and further work. Ultimately though, preparation work is only the beginning of a long journey into the irrevocable changes required when children are placed in new families.

4

The preparation of foster parents through the use of groups
Chris Fines

The traditional method of assessing foster parents on an individual basis often meant that whilst the local authority felt they knew sufficient about a family to approve them as foster parents at the end of the process, the family themselves often felt totally unprepared for the complex and difficult task which lay ahead. Moreover, the experience of this process of vetting on a very individual and personal level often resulted in a relationship between the local authority and the family where the local authority was seen as the expert and the family seen merely as providers of a resource. Emphasis on the family's own past experiences rather than their current situation also fed into a concept of foster parents as 'clients' rather than members of a child care team. The way in which foster parents are prepared and assessed seems to have a direct correlation with the way in which they subsequently see themselves and their relationship with the local authority. The model used for preparation and assessment provides the model for future work. The following is based on my experience of a series of groups designed to test out a model of combined assessment and preparation of foster parents through the use of groups.

The development and rationale of the group approach

When Westminster's Community Fostering Scheme was set up to provide family placements for difficult adolescents in 1979 it was still a new concept. It was therefore felt that if it was to be successful then a new approach was necessary to train and prepare the families who were the cornerstone of its implementation. A programme of group meetings for prospective families was developed based on the idea that everyone involved in the venture had both something to learn and something to contribute, and that if the assessment, training and preparation of the families was undertaken as a partnership, then the eventual placement of the adolescent would be undertaken in the same spirit. We believed preparation should be a process, not an event, and the structure of weekly groups with a period in between for contemplation and further work lent itself well to this idea. It was also hoped that given enough information and an opportunity to test out their own feelings and responses, the families concerned would be in a position to make their own assessment of whether they were suited to the task in hand. The social workers aimed to work with prospective families to evaluate their suitability rather than asking families to provide information to be interpreted and assessed by the social worker making a decision on the family's behalf. The Kent family placement project (Hazel and Cox 1976) had already demonstrated that group work could provide an effective method of selection and training, giving others the confidence to be more imaginative in their practice.

Group meetings were supplemented by individual visits to cover some of the issues in more detail and to afford an opportunity to discuss in private any issues which had arisen during the course of the groups or through the taking up of statutory references. It also provided an opportunity to see families in their own homes and to gain a more individual perspective. These home visits took place after families had formally applied to the scheme. Initially this could be done at any point, but in order to link practice to the theory that the groups were a process of learning and development, application forms were not given out until half-way through the series in later groups. By this time the programme had developed in such a way that the first half of the group meetings dealt broadly with issues which we hoped would enable both foster parents and workers to assess their suitability for the scheme, while the second half addressed the placement process.

The preparation groups were usually part of a recruitment campaign and were planned some time in advance. After initial telephone contact with social workers in the scheme, families were invited to an information meeting. This gave a chance for people to participate in a general information-giving session and provided an opportunity to ask questions at an early stage. The purpose and content of the preparation groups was explained at this meeting and families were given a programme to take away to look at before committing themselves to preparation groups. We stressed that the preparation groups did not commit people, but should they wish to proceed further and formally apply to join the scheme, they would need to have been to the majority of groups. It was also stressed that both partners should come to any meetings as we saw fostering as a venture for the whole family rather than the province of any individual family member. Families were encouraged to bring any children to as many of these sessions as they felt appropriate. Indeed many of the families' own children made very valuable and stimulating contributions to the sessions.

Design and content

The format and content of the sessions changed significantly over time and in many ways some of the earlier sessions belied the original theory behind using groups. We had wanted foster parents to be actively involved in the process and for their input to directly influence the mood and the content of group meetings. However, we organized the earlier sessions in such a way that they could only take a passive role and react to presentations rather than affording an opportunity for participants to contribute to and influence the sessions. Outside speakers were often called in to run the sessions, which were timetabled in a way which left little space for spontaneous developments. We simply replaced the model of local authority experts with the notion of outside experts, reinforcing the idea that there was a body of knowledge which could be 'taught', and clear precepts to pass on. This approach did not sit comfortably with our declared aims of developing a learning partnership, and was largely a reflection of an initial lack of confidence and a lack of familiarity with experiential training methods.

Over time the sessions developed along the experiential model and the commitment to seeing foster parents as equal members of the child care team was reflected in the fact that eventually all preparation groups were run with at least one foster parent as a co-leader. We designed sessions in a way which enabled the participants to generate their own material through exercises and small and large group discussions. We used the participants' experience of role-play and life drama to provide live material, and began to develop confidence in working with a framework which could be adapted to the here and now. The evolution of a more experiential approach coincided with contact with the National Foster Care Association Parenting Plus material which reinforced and legitimized our own feelings about the way in which we should be approaching the preparation groups. We had already adapted our preparation sessions to relate to adolescents and experience of the NFCA's 'Added to Adolescence' courses enabled us to refine and develop our programme. Sessions on issues such as identity and development were held against the backdrop of adolescence being a time of confusion and change, and we tried to explore the complex divide between behaviour which might occur as a natural part of growing up and behaviour which might be symptomatic of more deep-seated problems.

Fears of experimentation were particularly pertinent in relation to adolescents, and issues about the adolescents' own rights in regard to self-learning were very real. Foster parents wishing to lead the preparation groups attended the 'Added to Adolescence' courses and found this a very valuable way of preparing to lead the preparation groups. The concept of adult learning played an important role in the way in which material was presented and we continually tried to be aware that our role was to create an enabling environment and to provide information from which people could learn, rather than to lecture or attempt to teach families. It was also felt important to acknowledge each individual person's experience and views and not to get into a situation where responses and opinions were seen as right or wrong. There was a strong emphasis on enabling people to link their own experiences to the task we were preparing them for and a strong emphasis on what people had learnt from their past and how they had developed through it, rather than making judgements on the experience or event itself. Small group discussion featured prominently in the programme to enable people to explore ideas more fully in a group of people where size was not prohibitive. Role-play was used to enable people to get in touch with how situations made them feel and also to provide an opportunity to practise responses and reactions in a safe environment. Re-naming, 'role-play' and 'life drama' often made a great deal of difference to people's willingness to participate in this method of learning.

By the time preparation meetings began, it was hoped that having received booklets and literature on the scheme and attended the information meeting, potential foster parents would have a good general idea of what the scheme entailed. However, some time was allowed at the first preparation meeting for further questions. The first meeting concentrated on bringing people together as a group and looking at motivation in order to explore people's reasons for wanting to join the scheme. We set out the department's expectations of community foster parents at this initial session in order to lay down the boundaries. When looking at motivation, it was stressed that we were not looking for 'identikit' foster parents who would all have the same reasons for wanting to foster adolescents. This was also an opportunity to cut through some of the stereotypes of 'good' foster parents.

In this particular scheme the workers felt that it was not enough to be loving and warm and able to offer someone a home. Bearing in mind the tasks people would be undertaking, they needed other qualities, such as resiliance and determination. When looking at motivation we also looked at the fact that particular motives could be seen as good or bad depending on where they fitted into a complex range of motives. For instance, it was important that potential foster parents saw the undertaking as in some ways being similar to a job of work and, therefore, it was quite reasonable for people to be motivated by the fact that the scheme was fee-paying. However, if potential foster parents saw only a job with a reward element then this in itself was not enough. The first session ended with a look at some of the adolescents already placed in the scheme to begin to give people a picture of teenagers we were trying to place. We wanted to introduce an element of reality into this initial session and it was very helpful to have foster parents co-leading the sessions who were able to talk to profiles of the adolescents in a very real and meaningful way.

The second session looked at adolescent behaviour and started with exercises to enable potential foster parents to recall their own adolescence. People arrived for this session with a tape already playing in the background of music which would have been current during their teenage years. The walls were decorated with up-to-date teenage magazines and charts of the current top ten. The evening began with a guided fantasy involving a trip down memory lane whereby people were talked through their adolescent years and asked to recall some of their most significant moments. People were then divided into groups to do an exercise asking 'has the world changed?' This involved looking at various topics, e.g. education, discipline and employment, with a view to how things had changed since their adolescence. Linking these two exercises together enabled people to reflect on the fact that there were a lot of similarities between the questions and issues that preoccupied them as teenagers and those which occupy today's teenagers. Most participants, however, did feel that today's teenagers were subject to a great deal more pressure than they had been themselves. The evening moved on to look at when difficult adolescent behaviour was normal and when it was a problem. We used a monopoly game to look at this with a chart on the wall showing a behaviour range from pleasing to disturbing. There was a selection of cards for people to pick up with various behaviours written on them, many of them duplicates. People took a card in turn and placed it on the wall according to where they felt the behaviour should be and how they viewed it. Thus, having lots of noisy friends may be pleasing to some people, whilst it would be disturbing to others. This enabled people to start to get in touch with their own reactions to specific behaviour. Participants discussed the fact that for the majority of people some behaviours were seen in very much the same vein, e.g. drug taking was disturbing. People also discussed the question of degree and the fact that while a certain type of behaviour exhibited occasionally, e.g. withdrawing to a bedroom, may not be disturbing in itself, it would be disturbing if it was a constant occurrence. This exercise was designed to examine grey areas and to begin to promote an awareness of the fact that one could not always be categorical about whether a certain type of behaviour was normal or a problem and that one needed to look at the circumstances in which it occurred and its frequency. The evening ended with people being asked to look at what difficulties, habits and mannerisms they could tolerate and not tolerate.

In the early sessions couples were always divided up into different groups and this was one of several exercises where couples realized during the feedback sessions that they understandably had differing views which they might not have previously discussed. Again the emphasis was on the fact that the most significant thing about looking at what behaviour people could tolerate or not tolerate was becoming aware of their own reactions, rather than dividing the difficulties themselves into ones which people should be able to tolerate and ones which they should not. We were also able at this early stage to make people aware of some problems they would invariably have to tackle. For instance, virtually all the adolescents could be expected to stay out late at night at some point or to run off. We were also able to introduce the idea that the adolescents were most likely to pick up on the behaviour people found difficult and exhibit this very early on, and we asked people to look at how they would, in fact, deal with behaviour they said they could not tolerate. Again the foster parents were able to describe how this was experienced in reality and also to explain that when they had actually undertaken the work, they had often been surprised at the difference between what they thought they could tolerate and not tolerate and what actually happened. For instance, one particular family had been very concerned about glue sniffing, but in the event of having to deal with it, had dealt with it very capably, but had found themselves irritated to the extreme by the adolescent helping himself to food without asking.

The third session looked at development and identity and the concept of adolescence as a time of change. It also introduced the idea of the added element for adolescents in care and the fact that anxieties and uncertainties experienced by all adolescents tended to be heightened for those in care. The question of identity was explored and the fact that many elements of identity which people generally took for granted could pose problems for some of the adolescents we would be placing, e.g. friends. Many of the adolescents lacked experience in forming positive relationships, and whilst the fear of teenagers being led astray by friends was a reality, very often they did not have the skills and self-confidence to develop friendships. Many people gain a sense of self through their employment and when the scheme began, helping teenagers find the right employment was often a focal task. This became more difficult over time as unemployment developed as a national problem and opportunities became scarce. This session also looked at race and culture and people played a game whereby one group were given language and culture and had to attempt to communicate with another group who were given a different language and culture. This was a very helpful way of getting people in touch with the frustrations which can occur when people are operating without any understanding or knowledge of each other's core values. We confronted racism which developed as an issue over time alongside the development of the scheme's norms. We believed that all the foster parents in the scheme should be aware of the issue of racism, regardless of whether they were planning to take adolescents from different races and cultures or not and that, if they were to be *in loco parentis* to the adolescents placed, they should prepare them to live in a multi-racial society. Our success in recruiting black foster parents focused our attention on these issues and also provided an opportunity for us to understand more fully the effects of racism through their experience.

The fourth session looked at teenage problems and issues of communication. People were asked to role-play various situations which illustrated ways in which communication can become blocked and did exercises in active listening. For example, an adolescent may say 'my hair looks horrible and I feel fat'. If they receive the reply 'what do you want to look like, a film star?' the conversation may end there. What they may want to discuss is how they feel about themselves as a person, and negative comments on their appearance may be an opening gambit. This session looked at problems which frequently arose in placement and again the foster parents were able to give very graphic accounts of some of the situations people might expect to face. The session ended with a look at facilitating change and helping teenagers to like themselves as an antidote to the complex web of problems which people could expect to tackle.

The fifth session looked at personal and sexual relationships. Again participants were encouraged to look back to their own experiences particularly in relation to the development of their views on sex and sexuality.

The sixth session concentrated on the department's expectations of foster parents and the department's responsibilities. Some time was spent looking at the legal framework but there was a heavier emphasis on why teenagers came into care, to facilitate an understanding of their present problems. The concept of teamwork, and the model of foster parents and the social services department working together as a team, with differing but equally valid roles to play in planning and caring for the adolescents, was promoted. The importance of the undertaking being a venture for the whole family was stressed, and the concept of the family working as a team was explored using role play to highlight problems which can occur if couples allow themselves to be split. The acting out of a situation whereby one partner had given an adolescent a pound when the other had already refused it, enabled people to look at the degree of anger and tension which a seemingly small incident can generate. The assessment process was explained so that people were aware of the process they would go through if they decided to formally apply to the scheme.

The seventh session looked at placements and contracts. Each placement was made on a contract basis with an initial contract meeting, an end of contract meeting and three-monthly contract reviews in between. The adolescents were expected to participate fully in any meetings as part of the process of becoming responsible for themselves and their future. The contract was seen as a basis for negotiation and review and the tool by which the progress of the placement could be assessed and the goals and aims of the placement evaluated and redefined as appropriate. This session ended with rules and limits and an attempt to heighten people's awareness of the fact that generally they did not have enforceable rules and limits, their main tool being the relationship they were able to develop with the adolescent placed. This was directly contrasted to people's experience with their own children, who were usually well aware of the rules and boundaries that existed either explicitly or implicitly within the home, and could sense when they had reached the limit. This concept was one of the most difficult to communicate to potential foster parents and was often only truly appreciated once an adolescent was in placement.

The eighth and last session looked at endings. Because the scheme operated on the basis of time-limited placements ending when the adolescent reached 18, it was felt important to look at the concept of endings in the preparatory stage. This was linked to positive planning and ways in which foster parents could help the adolescent plan for a future of independence. Potential foster parents were asked to do an exercise looking at the conclusions they had reached for themselves about the sorts of teenagers they felt best able to help and it was hoped by this point they would have a fairly good understanding of their own strengths and weaknesses. They were asked to do this in their family units by identifying what they could offer and who might make best use of their family's life style. This was fed back to the larger group who contributed their own observations, either reinforcing or questioning the families' perceptions. The preparation meetings were reviewed as a whole and people were reminded of the complex and detailed range of topics they had covered.

The group process

Whilst each set of groups eventually followed very much the same format and content, each series took on its own identity and was experienced differently by the workers concerned. This was a reflection of the members of each group and their differing contributions to both the content of the groups and the group process. Individual members of the group took on different roles, e.g. each group had its joker and challenger. Feedback from the small groups to the large group was often undertaken by the same person and in later groups the workers encouraged everyone to take on this role, particularly since it provided a good model for later experience when families would be expected to participate in meetings concerning the adolescents placed. Because of the emphasis on the validity of each person's contributions, and the worker's avoidance of judging or assessing contributions to the group, there were times when group participants were unclear of the norms of the scheme. For example, it emerged on the individual assessment of one couple that they had very seriously considered dropping out of the scheme because their views were not in line with those of a particularly vociferous group member. They had taken the fact that the views articulated by this person had not been challenged to mean that they were acceptable, and thought there was, therefore, a fundamental conflict between their own views and the norms of the scheme. This particular experience led us to realize that, whilst we should continue to accept each person's views and experience as valid, we must also make clear the ground rules and the norms and culture of the scheme. This also helped people to evaluate themselves as it was clear for some people that their fundamental beliefs and attitudes were in direct conflict with the basic norms of the scheme, making it impossible for them to participate.

Despite the element of assessment in the groups, people appeared open and honest. There was rarely a sense that contributions were made with the workers in mind. An atmosphere of constructive criticism and debate developed which formed the basis for healthy ongoing debate between workers and foster parents. During the course of the preparation groups the participants came together as a group and developed a group identity. This was an important part of preparation for the support groups which they would later be required to join as part of the scheme. This caused problems when the scheme expanded and it was not possible to form new groups for each set of participants, as people found it difficult to split up into different support groups at the end of the preparation process. Usually, even those who did not eventually participate in the scheme saw the preparation meetings as useful and informative. Many foster parents said that it was hard to truly accept the scale of the difficulties they would face until an adolescent was placed with them, but that it was useful then to look back on the experience of the preparation groups.

During the process of becoming committed to the scheme the potential foster parents began to identify with the adolescents involved and the workers were often said to be too negative in their descriptions of the adolescents. However, most felt that having been prepared for the worst they were better able to deal with difficulties, although inevitably people had to cope with things we did not foresee. Having foster parents as co-leaders in the preparation groups was invaluable and there is no doubt that their contribution had a very profound and lasting effect on potential participants. People were also able to see, despite the very realistic portrayal by the foster parents of the difficulties and problems they could anticipate, that there was a lot to be gained from the undertaking.

Evaluation of the group approach

My own experience is echoed by others, and using the group method of preparation is now widely accepted as an effective method of preparing foster parents. In 1975 the National Foster Care Association set up a working party to study issues related to education and training in foster care and one of their conclusions was that social workers should spend more time and effort on long-term support of foster parents, rather than concentrating on selection and then wondering why so many placements broke down (NFCA 1977). We felt that such long-term support would be most effective when built on a foundation of adequate preparation. A survey of special fostering schemes undertaken by the London Boroughs' Regional Planning Committee (1982) found that all the schemes required foster parents to undergo a period of training at some point in the assessment process. Similarly, Shaw and Hipgrave (1983) found in their review of specialist fostering that three-quarters of the schemes surveyed provided specific training courses for specialist foster parents and that a number of them emphasized the applicants' commitment in response to the programme as a test of their suitability. They also found that seven out of ten of the agencies surveyed acknowledged that the relationship between foster parents in specialist schemes and the agency was different to that experienced by other foster parents. It was felt that training was a factor in this differing relationship. From the consumer's viewpoint, Crowley (1982) found that there were differences in attitude towards their preparation for the task between trained and untrained foster parents. For example, she found that two-thirds of those who had not attended a course saw themselves as ill-prepared for their role, whereas 95 per cent of the trained foster parents felt they had been prepared. Significantly, the latter also felt more positive about the vetting process. One of the foster parents in the Cheshire Family Placement Scheme (1982) felt that 'be prepared' should be the foster parents' motto: it does seem that, whilst many foster parents feel there is no substitute for actually doing the task, an attempt to thoroughly consider the issues and problems they may face with others in a similar position helps to develop confidence. The debate about specialist fostering schemes versus other forms of fostering will no doubt continue, but as McWhinnie (1978) has pointed out, training and group support is wanted and needed by all foster parents. One would hope that the positive advantages experienced by specialist schemes in the use of groups for preparation and training will continue to be offered to all foster parents and not just to those involved in specialist schemes.

SUMMARY

My own experience of using groups has led me to see it as a very valuable method of preparing potential foster parents for the increasingly difficult and complex job they are asked to do. Combining the preparation and assessment of foster parents in such groups does throw up some problems mentioned earlier, but the gains far outweigh any potential difficulties. The group process itself undoubtedly sets the model for working with the agency which, if based upon mutual support and development, can lead to the establishment of a team of workers in which foster parents play a key and valued role.

5

Groupwork in a multi-cultural setting

Ottis Edwards, Cecily Griffith and Beryl Jefferies

BACKGROUND

This chapter discusses how the fostering and adoption agency of an inner London borough has developed its skills in groupwork with black families who are interested in offering substitute homes to children. This is considered in the context of growing racial awareness in the agency. It recognizes that growth in knowledge and understanding of issues concerning race, racism and culture is an essential tool in this area of work and is relevant throughout social work practice. As an example of the agency's work, a preparatory parents' group of predominantly black applicants is described in some detail.

The authority is situated in inner London and has a large Afro-Caribbean community. It has a written child-care policy which emphasizes planning for children in care. The main thrusts of this policy are: 1) the prevention, if possible, of reception into care; 2) rehabilitation within the natural family as soon as possible; and 3) placement in a permanent substitute family of the child's own race. Underpinning this policy on fostering and adoption is the authority's equal opportunities policy and its anti-racist strategies. All these factors have contributed to the growth of knowledge and the development of child-care practice within the adoption and fostering unit.

INTRODUCTION

In the last ten years or so groupwork, as a method of preparing, selecting and supporting substitute families, has become more widely used than ever before. During the same period various training programmes have also been produced by national bodies which, although well structured and interesting, are inevitably written from a white perspective. The black perspective is either marginalized or forgotten. Some of these programmes are currently being revised to take account of this deficiency. We need to recruit black families for black children and, to achieve this, a sound knowledge of black culture and lifestyle is crucial. We have to be aware of the stress which black families face through living in a predominantly white society. It is also vital to understand the institutionalized racism within society and to acknowledge one's personal racism. All white social workers need to be aware of these issues. A blinkered approach will divorce social workers from the reality of the multicultural society in which we all live. More important, if we fail to consider these issues we shall put at greater risk those isolated children and black families who need help and shall not be able to help and prepare families who are receiving into their own family a child who has lived in a multi-racial community. Agencies who work regularly with black families will have experienced situations when white social workers who are racially unaware have exposed unconscious racism when meeting with a black family for the first time. This commonly shows itself as patronizing behaviour and stereotyping attitudes when they are meeting to discuss the requirements of a black child needing a family. The transition from this racially unaware and offensive attitude to one of confident understanding does not happen without will and determination.

The progress within our agency has taken place over a number of years. There has been a self-examination, at times painful and distressing, which in turn has lead to growth and deeper understanding of the meaning of institutional and personal racism. Once an understanding of the issues is achieved, a total commitment to own-race placement becomes a matter of good practice and is an expectation rather than an option. With this commitment comes the drive to recruit black families and to work effectively with black children.

In looking at this change, we can recognize various stages reached by those involved in the current debates on race placement. Firstly, there is a wide gap between intellectually accepting that own-race placement is a good thing, if you can find the right family, and the level of awareness where it becomes an unambiguous right of a black child to be cared for within the black community. Between these two stages there is much room for sabotage in achieving the stated goal.

Secondly, it is vital to listen to and believe what black people are saying about the disadvantages and oppression which they are facing.

Remember that black people speak from their own daily experience. It is a different experience from that of white people. They experience prejudice and discrimination in virtually every aspect of their lives, whether in work, education, housing or whatever. If black people protest about their circumstances, about negative stereotypes, use of offensive words, or institutionalized racism, we must listen and learn to adjust our own attitudes and give up some of our power. If we can do this, we shall develop a greater respect and regard for the integrity of the black person. We shall recognize the strength that has to be developed in the struggle, be able to share the anger felt by the black community and also be able to challenge the racist assumptions made when these concerns are blandly dismissed on the radio, television and other media, or by colleagues, friends and family.

Thirdly, we must be aware of the meaning of the word 'black' and use it with confidence. And we must be aware that children who have one white and one black parent will be perceived as black people by white society. These children of mixed parentage will experience racism and it is essential, therefore, that they develop a strong black identity. Many social workers find it very difficult to accept these children as black. They do not understand that the part of the children's identity which is white will be reinforced by almost every aspect of society and be unconsciously confirmed all the time. It is their black identity which must be strong, because this is the identity which society gives to them.

Our attitudes will change if we are willing to expose ourselves to these factors. Such changes will be greatly helped if, as in our agency, more black staff are employed and there are clear expectations from the local authority and management. Access to black colleagues has been a major influence on attitudes in the section and it is within this context of change that groupwork has developed within the agency.

Groupwork

Groupwork, within the agency, has been used as a method of preparation and support for substitute families at least since 1980. The content of the preparatory groups has been influenced by the agency's written child-care policy which led to a more sophisticated understanding of the concepts of: 1) task-centred or contract fostering with the aim that the child would be moving on, with rehabilitation as the first option; and 2) permanent parenting, where the plan is for the child to remain within the substitute family, with adoption as a first option.

In the early 1980s a groupwork consultant was appointed to the department and two training packs were developed as a basic tool for the social workers and foster parents who ran the preparation groups. In those early days it was common to say that black families would not attend groups and that perhaps we needed to modify our expectations of group attendance to make the process easier for black applicants.

In fact, this has not in any way happened. The most significant alteration in the way we run groups concerns subtler changes. These reflect the fact that workers have started to face their own unconscious racism and also the fact that membership and leadership of the groups are now racially balanced. Apart from groups arising from specific campaigns, membership of the groups is virtually always racially mixed. Permanent-parenting groups, however, tend to have a higher proportion of white applicants while task-centred fostering groups commonly have a higher proportion of black applicants.

The preparatory groups are usually run with two co-leaders. These are usually social workers, although fostering groups have sometimes been co-led with a foster parent and this has been extremely successful. A recent change has been the insistence that the leadership comprised at least one black worker.

The selection of co-leaders is very important. In the co-running of groups, it is essential for the group leaders to work well together and to have a mutual regard for each other. The use of our groupwork consultant to enable new leaders to do some co-working exercises before setting up the groups is invaluable. These exercises will allow the sharing between the workers of any fears, fantasies or annoyances that they may hold about the other. They also help to resolve issues concerning such things as dominance and sharing of leadership styles, they clarify the purpose of the groups, and are an opportunity to reinforce the aspects in which each person is most skilled.

When running groups with one black and one white leader there may be unconscious attitudes suggesting that authority and power rest with the white worker. It is essential, therefore, to lead the group in such a manner that such attitudes are challenged rather than reinforced. Co-working is a positive method of leading these groups. It allows effective teamwork and yet permits us to disagree sometimes while retaining mutual respect. If tension and disharmony develop between the co-workers, this will sabotage the group, who will immediately recognize any conflict.

Preparation groups

The aim of the fostering and permanent-parenting groups is to prepare applicants by allowing them to look at some of the issues in depth. Applicants can then consider more clearly whether this type of care is right for them and their family.

We generally arrange the groups to run one evening per week for five or six weeks consecutively at a central venue with good access to public transport. Each session will last at least 90 minutes. We endeavour to have a rolling programme of groups throughout the year.

Occasionally we arrange week-end workshops for those applicants who cannot easily attend during the evening because they are single parents or do evening work. The disadvantages of week-end groups are: 1) that only a limited amount of information can be absorbed in a day; 2) they do not give applicants a chance to mull over issues and reflect them back later; and 3) much learning comes through discussion of personal experience and feelings and it takes two or three sessions to build up a level of trust where applicants share their personal feelings.

In most respects, the basic programmes of the groups for permanent parenting and for foster parenting have changed little over the years and do not differ from those described by other contributors in this Section. The one big change lies in the manner in which racial and cultural considerations are dealt with. Five or six years ago, when the programme was devised, 'cultural issues' used to be a specific topic (rather like Life-story Work or Going to Court). At that time, the focus tended to be on the things which white carers needed to know and be aware of in looking after black children. Now, however, racial and cultural considerations are a theme which runs through the entire programme.

This is achieved by setting the scene in the first session when we explain the agency's child-care policy. By this policy, the thrust of a social worker's efforts is concentrated on: firstly, prevention of reception into care; secondly, rehabilitation back to the natural family as quickly as possible; and lastly, if all else fails, placement in a permanent substitute family of the child's own race. This scene-setting immediately gives an opportunity for discussion about the reasons for the agency's policy on own-race placement and the applicants' reaction to it.

In further sessions, we look at the special needs of children who have been in care. Arising from the experiences of these children, the opportunity arises to look at the way in which black children can come to devalue their race and culture and to highlight the reasons why restoration to a black family is the only really effective means of reversing this process.

We also ask black applicants to challenge their fears about parenting a child with a 'mentally ill' parent. (There are an exceptionally large number of children on referal who have parents described as 'mentally ill'.) Some professionals may have difficulty in reaching clear assessments if they are unfamiliar with the culturally different ways of expressing emotions. In the groups, we consider the possibility of unconscious racism in all this. We ask applicants to think about the impact on young parents of having to cope with the effects of racism whilst being away from the extended family and from their roots. We ask them to take all these factors into account when considering mental illness.

Both with permanent-parenting and foster-parenting preparation groups, we aim to run a rolling programme of groups through the year so that, at any one time, applicants do not have to wait for more than eight weeks for a group. Those invited to attend the groups will all have had some individual contact with the agency. They will also have been visited at home in order to ascertain whether they seem to have the potential capacity for the type of care which they are considering. A decision whether or not to proceed beyond this initial contact is only made after discussion with social workers in the section. If we decide not to proceed, we give clear reasons to the applicant, in writing.

For all groupwork, training and consultation must be available. A borough-wide scheme for groupwork training and consultation has been developed within the borough. The need for black groupwork consultants has also become more evident as groupwork has developed within the agency. In the same way that our black colleagues have been able to help white colleagues understand and face issues of personal and institutional racism, so a black groupwork consultant is particularly able to help groupworkers to understand, and more effectively to deal with, the dynamics of racism in the groups. White colleagues must not expect, however, that, because a black person is involved, the responsibility for issues of race and racism is passed to that person. The advice and consultation are to help the worker deal personally with the racism and recognize their own part in it. If white social workers do not have the advantage of working directly with black colleagues on a daily basis, then it is advisable to seek a black consultant.

The preparation groups and support groups described here represent only part of the groupwork with black families that is being undertaken by the agency. Most of the groups are mixed groups of black and white families, although occasionally there have been groups consisting entirely of black families. To work effectively in this way with black families, it is important to hold all the skills necessary for groupwork and to have access to training and consultation. A crucial additional ability is to be racially aware and to recognize personal and institutionalized racism.

With this awareness and a true commitment to Britain as a multi-cultural society, race and culture can become a central theme in the groups. The awareness will only be achieved if white social workers allow themselves to recognize their own part in racism in society. This uncomfortable, but essential, recognition will lead to personal growth and to better professional practice.

A PERMANENT-PARENTING GROUP OF PREDOMINANTLY BLACK APPLICANTS

Here we describe in some detail a group run for permanent parents, the majority of whom were black. The objectives of such groups, as already hinted, are preparation and training with a view to selection and recruitment. In more detail the groups aim to:

Provide adoptive parents with an understanding of the kinds of children that are in care and awaiting substitute families. This means exploring in depth the effect which the children's backgrounds and experiences will have on their behaviour and looking at how this manifests itself in their attitude, development, self-awareness and sense of racial identity.

Enable families to analyse their motivation for becoming substitute parents and to help them form a realistic approach to their own hopes, fears and expectations.

Examine and explore their parenting capacity and to help them look back on their relationship with their own parents and discover how this has, or will, influence them as parents.

Provide information on current issues and how the agency works; introduce the families to a positive working relationship with the agency; assess their families' present understanding of the tasks involved and their ability, willingness and understanding of the need to work in partnership with the agency.

Thus, the purpose was to train, prepare and select new families predominantly for black children, some of whom were previously cared for by white carers in residential establishments or in foster homes.

How the group was set up

The families in this group were all interested in permanent parenting and every group member was invited by a groupwork officer and seen by a social worker. The group consisted of about 20 members at the start and the majority were black; some members were single while some were couples (either mixed in race or black) and there was a wide range of age and background. By the second week the numbers had fallen to 14 and continued to decline to about 10 by the time the group ended. The venue was accessible with good public transport and meetings were held in the evenings from 7.00 to 9.30 pm. The group was run by two black social workers with a wide knowledge of adoption and fostering. Both are committed to helping children and placing them in families where they can be assisted to develop a sound, healthy racial identity.

Techniques used: In each session we introduced games and exercises as a technique. For example, in our first session we felt it was particularly important to break the ice and create a feeling of relaxation.

In the 'Getting to know you' exercises, each group participant worked as one of a pair with the person next to them (not with their permanent partner). Each member of the pair talked to the other for two minutes and the results were then fed back to the group. From the outset it seemed that people were very willing to share information about themselves, as was revealed by the individual feedback. We noticed how highly motivated people were. We later came to recognize that this particular exercise of sharing information laid the foundation for what was to come.

The 'name game' exists in various versions but we chose one which was particularly effective in helping members to locate themselves in terms of their roots, personal identity and racial identity. Each member said their names and then concentrated on sharing how they got them, what the name meant and how important it was to them. Most members felt their names were very important to them. They did not appreciate it when members of their different establishments or work places chose not to try to get to know their unfamiliar-sounding names. Thus one group worker recalled that for several different periods of her life, employers and colleagues re-named her, so to speak, so that she had had contact with literally thousands of people who never knew her real name. Several members reported the same experiences.

There are two important remarks to be made about this sort of denial of identity: First, our name is a crucial part of our identity, personal as well as cultural. There are so many black men who have been named 'John', 'Dave', and 'Tom' and similarly black women dubbed 'Mary', 'Sally' etc., to replace unusual-sounding African, Asian or West Indian names. Second, children who are to be fostered or adopted have already been named, and, as we recognized earlier, the names are part of their identity. Therefore any attempt by new parents to suppress or change these names will be actually an attempt to deny part of the child's identity. There may be a rare occasion when a child of the adoptive family has the same name as the new child, but these can be dealt with by adding another name.

The name game also helped members to talk about their family background and their parents' life-style. Some members were able to tell about the thinking behind their parents' choice of name, e.g. some names meant 'a gift from God'. It is also interesting that one member, who is now a social worker, discovered that her own name meant 'one who listens'.

Apart from distortion and pseudo-names, another severance and alienation that the black person encounters is having to live with imposed names. For example, all the black people in the group were aware that their present surnames did not indicate their family line, since their original names had been taken from their fore-parents and replaced during the slavery and plantation era.

We took great pains to avoid using the term 'mixed race', because it is, in itself, racist – the inference being that one partner is white. No such distinction is made concerning marriages where the partners differ only in national origins. Both for the couples themselves, and for the children born of such couples, we always used the term 'mixed parentage' rather than 'mixed race'. As already pointed out, children who come from mixed relationships are, in fact, black children, because the society in which we live perceives them as being non-white. It is therefore important for them that their parents, schools and all concerned help them to build a positive black identity.

Many group members suggested that such divisions were just another aspect of racism, i.e. the divide-and-rule formula. The group explored how the children could have mixed racial loyalties if the predominant influences in their lives were white – for instance if they were of mixed parentage, growing up in white establishments, or in white, middle-class families having no contact with the black community. The group brainstormed a number of controversial ideas about a positive black self-image. One of these was the use of the word 'black' in relation to themselves, instead of 'brown' or 'coloured'. One member, who had worked with children, reported that they describe themselves as 'brown' and not 'black'.

Task and contents: The tasks and contents were spread out over five sessions with each session examining different relevant aspects of parenting and child care.

Session 1 dealt with 'Who are the children in care?' It also examined the kind of experiences that they have had and, of course, planning for children in care.

Session 2 focused on parenting. In this session we tried to identify what these children would need from parents and, on the other hand, what the parents would have to offer. Consequently, applicants were more able to appreciate the type of child to whom they could become parents. This was, so to speak, a preliminary matching exercise although not theoretically such.

Session 3 concentrated on the child's arrival and the necessary adjustments that the family would have to make and how they would handle the child. We also considered what adjustments the child might have to make. The group had the opportunity to examine and analyse their hopes and expectations.

Session 4 was concerned with introducing the child to the family and with the issue of personal identity. Group members discussed how and where they would meet the child and how to talk to the child about his or her background, cultural issues, natural parents, past caretakers and significant other people. The child's need to understand its past and its background and to be able to talk about these are important parts of a fully integrated self-concept which, in turn, will produce a healthy personality.

Session 5, the final session, gave applicants the opportunity to solve unanswered questions and to move on to the next stage in the proceedings. Assessment and home study, legal procedures and working with the local authority and other affiliated agencies were also part of this discussion. In addition, the session looked at how applicants were feeling and what they had gained from the group. By the time the group had ended, all members were very motivated and eager to pursue the process of adoption.

The dynamics of the group

Two of the white members were male although it was also very clear that much of the vying for power and the struggle for leadership that emerged came from the white female member. The white female member also seemed inclined to dominate the group and always expressed the views of her husband and herself. He, although educated and articulate, tended to be silent, unless specifically drawn out, and even on such occasions he often held back. At one stage there was a real power struggle between two white members and the two black group workers as to which direction the group should take. The workers only managed to remain in control because of their facilitating skills. Their ability to work successfully together helped them to complete the task and to enable and maintain the group.

One black male partner, who took on the role of rescuer on several occasions, became popular with other group members. His partner seemed less confident than he was and this allowed her to join in while he spoke. One particular black female member held the group's attention on the few occasions when she spoke because of her excellent understanding of some of the children's behaviour.

Everyone in the group had experienced racism, and we were able to discuss this openly. Had there been more white members in the group, the group might have felt inhibited and less able to share such painful and sensitive experiences. Some exercises focused on how parents would deal with their children after they had been subjected to racial abuse by their peers in school.

To discuss this the group was split into pairs and each member of a pair talked to the other for about three minutes on how they would deal with a child who was subjected to racial abuse by its peers. After this the group began a general discussion on the topic and reported their own experiences. One member recalled how her five-year-old son had come home from school crying, having been called 'a black bastard who eats Kit-e-Kat' (popular cat food). Another member recalled that, when she had lived in a predominantly white neighbourhood, her son had been called 'the black sheep'. The child had been told that names could not hurt, but that if somebody hit him, that would be different. Others talked about their own experiences of racism. An ex-nurse had been told by a patient 'to take her black hands off him and go back to the bush'. These and other more subtle acts, including not wanting to associate with colleagues outside the work situation, were discussed. One of the group members talked about the distress caused to her daughter when she was about eight years old. In her class of 24 children every child except her was invited to a birthday party being given by one of the children. The child in question openly said that she could not invite any black friends because her parents would not allow it. According to the black child's parents, this not only lowered her self-esteem but affected her school performance. At school the following week the class had discussed what they had done during the previous week-end, and naturally the black child was alone in describing her different week-end.

How racism works and the effect it has on black people were illustrated by one member who said that her son, who had been born in England, first visited the West Indies when six years old and had remarked, on being introduced to his grandfather: 'Mum, he could never be my grandfather. He is too black.' This prompted group members to look at the effect which living in a predominantly white society was having on black children. Many children feel uncertain about their identity and, given the chance, some may reject everything that is black. Similarly, some black children living in residential establishments reject typical West Indian food. They take on the white culture in every aspect and view it as being the right and proper way. In looking for substitute families for our children we aim to find families who can help them with their racial identities.

As group leaders, we had several roles: to give information, to get the task done, and to maintain the group. At the start of the group, one of our most important tasks was to explain and debate the agency's policies and practices. We found that the most controversial of these was the authority's stance regarding transracial placements and equal opportunities. Some members were racially aware and could only perceive same-race placements as the right and proper thing to do in order to meet a child's racial needs. There were those who were less sure, mainly because they had not given much thought to the issue and, for some of these, it was the first time that they had had such an academic discussion on racism and its effects on its victims. Most of them, however, were fully aware of how it affected them in their day-to-day lives.

We needed to use all our knowledge and persuasive powers on some members who were indifferent, or opposed, or strongly opposed to placing black children only in black families. At the start, some of these felt that a child's needs could be met in any family and that such a family did not have to reflect the child's racial origin. The white member present took this view and some black members agreed with that person. This was a controversial subject and sparked off a lively debate. In our discussions we gave verbal profiles of children who were undergoing identity crises – for example, covering skin with lather or talcum powder or, at the other extreme, using razor blades to scrape off the epidermis and so try to identify with the white family in which they were placed.

Comments by the group workers: From a very early stage in the group we noticed that the dynamics were different to that of other groups which we had run in the past. This was a very lively and enjoyable group, eager to share, to learn and openly to discuss individual contributions. One explanation was that the dynamics of this predominantly black group, with a black leadership, were different from those of predominantly white groups we had run in the past.

The black participants were able to respect and value the group workers' role and position in the group. In reverse situations, white participants, because of their sometimes unconscious racism, found it difficult to accept any authority or leadership from a black person. Through their conditioning and process of socialization they had formed stereotypes about black peoples' ability to perform complicated tasks or to reach professional excellence in any field. In white groups, from past experience, those of us who are black always had to prove ourselves. And this sort of competitiveness was not of the healthy type. Credibility, trust and respect were more easily established in the black group because the group was not influenced or dominated by the dynamics of racism. Two of the white participants in this group demonstrated a tendency to trivialize any important points or themes, especially if these were being made in connection with black self-awareness and identity. For example, one member thought that basically the only serious problem with trans-racial adoptions was that 'it was unfair that black people now seem very determined to snatch the black children back to reclaim them'.

In any debate or argument for or against own-race placements, the above statement merely endorses the own-race policy and acknowledges that black children have been uprooted (if not 'snatched') from their racial and cultural roots, denying them their greatest human heritage. Such statements can only serve to confirm the arguments for own-race placements. On the positive side, the remark sparked off a lively discussion in the group, with group members addressing this very vexed question in a positive way and going on to explore the importance of a sound racial identity – a good healthy black identity.

We found that at the start, and in the early stages of the group, some black members who had white partners referred to their children as 'half caste' and some referred to themselves as being 'brown' and some as 'coloured'. By examining and analysing some of the perceptions they had of themselves, the group was able to explore the way that black people often collude with racism. Nevertheless, some members showed reluctance to accept the word 'black' and one person said she would always refer to her child as half-caste while she was at home.

This exploration and self-examination caused some people to drop out of the group. Others were able to see that words like 'brown', 'coloured', 'mixed-race' etc., were racist language and represented attempts to prevent black people having a feeling of great pride in their black identity.

SUMMARY

We have highlighted some of the elements of racism that affected the dynamics of the group. We would not wish to omit saying how positive the group was (by and large), how hard the members worked, how committed they were, how motivated they were and, generally, what a nice group they made. The honesty and trust were deep and their enthusiasm seemed unparalleled.

Running the group we found to be hard work, but this was rewarded by the members' interest, commitment and willingness to work very hard at exploring the needs of the children we have in care and what resources they could offer such children if they became substitute parents. Finally, we are appreciative and thankful for the support we have received from colleagues and to the group members whose contributions made this chapter possible.

ADDENDUM TO CHAPTER 5

Editor's Note

Because experience with Afro-Caribbean families is still in its early stages, the following contribution should be read as an addendum to the previous chapter. I am indebted for it to Pauline Wellington and Marie Ramdham who are social workers in Barnardo's London Division Homefinding Project, a multi-racial team of social workers seeking permanent family placements.

The experience of racism deters black families from approaching social work agencies which are still predominantly seen as white and middle class. Because of the past tendency on the part of agencies to look upon black families as not functioning well (i.e. not like the stereotype of the white family), not surprisingly prospective adoptive or foster families anticipate rejection. As one of our project foster parents put it: 'they don't feel quite worthy so they will back off before they get hurt'. It took black people a long time to accept that there were black children in care and to recognize that this may have been because of a breakdown in their parents' coping rather than as previously thought that they were 'taken away' by social workers. Because Social Services Departments saw black families as a problem and were perceived as destructive to black families, prospective applicants were reluctant to approach these same people to offer to care for a child. Past stereotypes also about black families often resulted in the rejection of those who did come forward offering to foster or adopt. Sometimes black families were offered child minding as a substitute for adoption and fostering.

While more recently the Barkingside Project has been working with young professional couples, in the past black applicants have tended to be older. They were members of the more established groups who had already brought up their own children. A number of families are in the age range of 50–70 but our experience is that they are successful in the fostering task, particularly with teenagers, some of whom may be presenting serious emotional and behavioural difficulties.

Relatively more black single women than white approach the Project. Among the black community in Britain, single black parents are unlikely to be isolated and there is little stigma. This is partly due to the pattern of family life imposed on black people in the West Indies by slavery and partly because of the contribution single people make at home. We feel strongly also the need to emphasize that unmarried couples are normally accepted by the Afro-Caribbean Community. Accommodation is often less spacious in black families, mainly because of the sort of housing available to them, their relatively lower income than white families and the comings and goings of adult children, relatives from the West Indies and so on. However, although a child joining a family may not have his or her own room, this does not seem to be a problem and recognition of the need for privacy is worked out. Shared care through the extended family network is a major strength of many black families and children are able to cope happily with a number of carers because of the close bond between those carers. In the words of our Panel Chair, acknowledging differences in the circumstances and culture of black applicants is 'in no way a lowering of standards but is acceptance of another equally valid way of family life'.

Recruitment

In recruiting black families, the 'grapevine' is very important, as is personal contact with churches and other groups. However, if it is necessary to advertise, there are weekly newspapers with an Afro-Caribbean readership. Adverts in the *Guardian* also attract black families. In advertising, it is important to be sensitive to the use of terminology. Some descriptions such as half caste, coffee coloured, very black are seen as derogatory. More acceptable terms include mixed parentage, Afro-Caribbean, black West Indian, Anglo/Afro/Caribbean.

In conveying the needs of children described, care must be taken not to offend with too much detail which focuses on problems or to use language which is unfamiliar or confusing, e.g. 'sexually aware', 'disturbed behaviour', 'enuresis', 'child guidance', 'psychotherapy'. It is preferable to talk personally to enquirers about such problems rather than describe them in advertisements.

Working with families: We know from our experience that white workers can work effectively with black families, but it is important that black and white workers work closely as a team. Sometimes black families can be stereotyped to their detriment. This includes statements such as: 'obsessed with work and religion', 'strict', 'athletic', 'musical' and 'educationally orientated'. As black workers, we have increased our skills and our expertise through discussion with our white colleagues and we in turn have been able to share our perspectives and our knowledge of black history and culture with them. We have also been able to acknowledge that we all have prejudices.

Working with a black family may take longer because of their need for reassurance that their offer will be understood and valued and the importance of explaining why personal and detailed information, and the involvement of wider family members, is required.

All families working with the Project are invited to and expected to participate in preparation groups, comprising four meetings attended by experienced adoptive and foster parents and residential social workers, as well as home-finding social workers and applicants. In our experience it is important for black as well as white families to attend groups, but we do not run special groups for black families. However, in order to help the family feel comfortable in the group, possibly several initial visits need to be made to the family and clear explanation given. Black families feel more secure if there are other black members in the group, especially black social workers. A number of black families are not used to groups and they are unsure what is expected of them. If a black social worker is there to be able to help them along when they want to raise a particular point they feel more confident. A myth that most people have about groups, whether they are black or white, is that you have to expose yourself, lay yourself bare, so that has to be clarified beforehand to ensure there is no pressure on people. The workers may have to be prepared to wait a long time for any input and must let people know that even if they are not actively contributing to the group their presence is still very much appreciated. We have found that families have gained good understanding of the issues discussed, even when they have not participated verbally.

Generally, black families seem to need more encouragement than white families before feeling confident about joining a group. As an alternative to several initial visits at home by a social worker who will be part of the group, it may be helpful for black families to have an opportunity to meet together beforehand. We have also found black families willing to attend and able to use post-placement support groups.

SUMMARY

It is our experience that Afro-Caribbean families are coming forward in greater numbers, initially for older children, but more recently for babies and toddlers. It is very important that we respond promptly and sensitively and with awareness of the historical, social and cultural context in which families are approaching us, so that black children can enjoy the best possible opportunities of fulfilling their potential.

Section 2

Using groups to prepare and support children

6

Introduction

John Triseliotis

A key social work aim with children in care is to help them sustain their identity whilst also preparing them for their next move. The move can be for a return home, placement with temporary or long-term foster parents, or with an adoptive family, or a move towards independent living in the community.

This kind of work involves the social worker becoming familiar with the child and his world, learning about his circumstances, interests, hopes and expectations, as well as his fears, anxieties and possible problems. A trustful relationship will have to be developed which will allow for meaningful communications, including planning and preparatory work to take place. This can be difficult because, as others have pointed out, many children are apprehensive, confused, puzzled and uncertain about what is happening to them and what the future holds for them. Separation from their families and social environment leaves many with feelings of distress and anxieties which frequently affect their capacity to settle down to develop new relationships. For example, many children cannot understand why they cannot live with their own families or are uncertain where they belong and unsure of their identity. Unlike other children, life holds too many unpredictables for them and being in care or foster care makes many feel different from other children. (See also Donley, 1981, and Jewett, 1984.)

Helping children in care to overcome personal and social difficulties and understand what has been happening to them requires of the social worker the capacity to communicate with children of different age groups. Yet without a sense of trust and safety having been developed between the two, deeply felt personal experiences are unlikely to be shared and participation in the process of planning may become artificial. Winnicott (1970), commenting on how children tend to withdraw or fail to respond to direct interviewing, adds that most children before they reveal themselves will want to see and experience the worker 'as a real person and to assess his or her attitudes and intentions'. Winnicott introduced the useful notion of the 'indirect approach' or of the 'third object' in work with children. In the majority of cases, she argued, 'it helps to have something between us and the child, a third thing going on which at any moment can become a focal point to relieve tension'. The 'third thing' can be a car ride, drawing, walking, the presence of a pet or playing games. Games offer the opportunity of starting with those that require few words, before introducing games or activities requiring longer exchanges. Donley (1981) and Jewett (1984) make additional useful suggestions about working with separated children at an individual level. The preparation of 'life story books' is another activity which performs the double function of putting the child in contact with its origins and circumstances and also helping to establish communication and build trust.

There are different techniques a worker can use to establish meaningful contact with children as a medium for carrying out desirable objectives, and groupwork offers an additional tool to more traditional casework methods. Groups can also be seen as 'the third thing' which facilitates communication with children, enabling them through discussion, games, exercises or role play to share their 'preoccupations, anxieties, frustrations and hopes'. Experience suggests that pre-adolescents, and also particularly adolescents and late teenagers, find it much easier to talk in a group of peers rather than in face-to-face interviews. The group is not meant to replace but to supplement individual work.

Previous examples of using groupwork with children in care, as opposed to group living, come almost exclusively from the USA. The groups are described as for children in 'foster care', but because of the American tendency to lump together residential and foster care, it is hard to distinguish at times what they are exactly referring to. The examples fall mainly into two groups: those for pre-adolescents (aged 8–12); and those for adolescents and teenagers (aged about 12–16). In these examples the group was seen mainly as a therapeutic tool offering to the children the opportunity to ventilate and reflect on feelings concerning their fostering status, their natural families, their future and on relationships with the agency and the social worker. It was also felt that the children's participation in these groups would make the task of the carers somewhat easier. There was no mention then of the group being used as a preparatory tool. The assumption would be that any child who participated in these groups and was helped to sort out his confusions, would also be in a better position to participate in and make use of a new move. An example of this is offered by Mullender on pages 127–139, Chapter 9. In Mullender's case the aim was to help black children placed with white foster parents to develop their racial and cultural awareness.

Underlying concepts: The American examples, to be described later, took place mostly in the 1960s and early 1970s when somewhat different kinds of practice preoccupations predominated and the objectives of group work had not yet been spelled out. The basic premise appeared to be that growing up in care and foster care can impinge on the children's emotional and social adjustment and particularly on the process of identity formation, especially during adolescence. Furthermore, that problems in identity formation and adjustment are usually related either to the circumstances of the children's separation from their families, and/or to the fact of being in care or foster care. (Later research was to show not only the high rate of emotional problems displayed by children in care and foster care but also to confirm the confusion, anger and frustration they feel about their circumstances and status. Page and Clark (1977), Triseliotis and Russell (1984), Rowe et al. (1984).) Though Wolkind and Rutter (1973) argue that many children appear to be severely damaged by their experiences prior to their admission into care, Triseliotis and Russell (1984) found evidence of how the in-care situation also adds to these problems.

Allowing for the elusiveness and complexity of defining identity and sense of self, nevertheless the literature, in some cases backed up by research, has identified a number of factors which can enhance or hold back identity formation for children in care and foster care. These include: the quality of relationships; communications about the children's 'in-care' circumstances; the children's feelings about their status and origins and their perceptions of community attitudes towards them. Whilst groupwork by itself can offer little to improve the quality of relationships the children are experiencing, it can contribute to the enhancement of their identity and adjustment by offering them a number of opportunities, some of them included in these early examples of groupwork. They include opportunities to reflect on current relationships; to gain better understanding about their overall in-care situation; to link their past life, current circumstances and futures; to place themselves in a social world; and provide them with some of the emotional resources and social skills necessary to cope with possible negative attitudes and to manage community living in general.

Groups for pre-adolescents: In contrast to those who say that 'latency' children cannot use groups, Sullivan (1953) claims this to be an important period of socialization, emphasizing 'chumship' in the development of interpersonal relationships. Hargrave and Hargrave (1983) in their summary of Sullivan's work, comment that this stage of personality development is characterized by the child submitting his or her emerging self-concept to the corrective interplay experienced in close interaction with peers. Sullivan goes even further, claiming that when a child sees himself or herself reflected through a peer's eyes, the experience can possibly heal the effects of earlier poor parenting and potentially prevent later serious emotional disturbance. Recent research has supported Sullivan's views about the importance of the pre-adolescent period in the development of peer relationships, including the ideas about friendships characteristic of this age group. (See Selman et al, 1977, Younis and Volpe 1978 and Forbes, 1978).

Watson and Boverman (1971) and Ludlow and Epstein (1972) provide possibly the first examples of groups being used for pre-adolescent foster children as a way 'to reach a fuller understanding of the unique problems faced by children growing up in foster care'. They saw the group as providing 'a medium in which foster children could talk about themselves and their environment'. Both types of groups excluded children with severe emotional problems and relied simply on discussion without activity. In spite of their young age, the children voiced feelings about themselves, their families and siblings, why social workers kept changing, etc. Overall they verbalized feelings of: *low self worth* (why am I not with my parents; why was I given up); *of dependency* (who will take care of me tomorrow); and of *identity* (who am I). It is claimed that as a result of their group experience, the children became more open with their social worker. Hargrave and Hargrave (1983) provide a more recent example of using a groupwork approach to the behaviour problems of pre-adolescents, though these were not in care. What the authors describe as their group therapy programme was designed to develop social skills and encourage personal interaction. This was to be achieved through a combination of discussion, activity and 'snacks'. Thus the writers appropriately accept that both discussion and activity can contribute towards therapy goals with children aged between 9 and 12. The authors go on to argue that at this stage groups composed of all boys or all girls work best to develop the 'chumship' types of relationships that are the goal of the programme. They see the operational size of the group as being between 8 and 10 children. Children referred to the group had to have problems of getting along with other children, either because of shyness, over-aggressiveness or hyperactivity.

Groups for adolescents: If there are some lingering doubts about the capacity of pre-adolescents to use groups, these do not exist in the case of adolescents and teenagers – quite the contrary. The theoretical proposition is that adolescents are striving to be part of a group and that they feel more at home in groups with peers and therefore find it easier to use each other and share thoughts and feelings. Early examples of using groupwork for adolescents in foster care are provided by Carter (1968) and Peterson and Sturgies (1971). The first describes a group of adolescent boys whilst the second is about a similar type of group for girls. The groups were then seen as a way of helping adolescents to solve their problems through the group method. Fortnightly meetings were held throughout a whole year. Like the group for pre-adolescents the children shared a lot of feelings about being labelled 'foster children' and about their general fostering situation, their natural and foster parents and about the agency that had control over them. The meetings were also used to share views and anxieties about relationships with peers and members of the opposite sex. 'Feelings of love and loneliness' were also voiced.

A more recent example from the USA is provided by Euster and others (1984) who found from a survey of child care workers in South Carolina that they saw a need for some foster children 'to learn appropriate peer interaction skills and experiences to help them to build their self-confidence, minimize feelings of being different from their peers and give them skills for making friends'. Euster et al. (1984) outline the following programme for their 'life skills groups':

Session 1 Feelings and perceptions about being fostered etc.
Session 2 Making friends – use of role play, games, puppets.
Session 3 Information about sex – use of films dealing with reproduc-

tion, contraception, venereal disease, teenage pregnancy (now possibly add AIDS).

Session 4 Sexuality – the ability to discuss and clarify personal values as well as to explore feelings about sex and marriage.

Session 5 Personal and relationship problem-solving; communication skills, assertiveness skills and stress control.

Though the above objectives may seem rather limited, the groupwork techniques that emerge are of group workers trying, through discussion, to gain acceptance by the children and to generate a sense of trust. Participants are also encouraged to share problems and experiences, and both positive and negative feelings about their situation. Sometimes the group leaders also initiated discussion about a particular theme, e.g. the family of origins. What is rather surprising is the absence in the various groupwork programmes described of any discussion around racial and cultural awareness, though many of the children in care in the USA are of black or Hispanic origin.

There is no evidence that, prior to the early 1970s, there was any consistent attempt in Britain to use groupwork techniques with children in care or with those on supervision from the Courts. The main impetus seems to have come, first, from the Children and Young Persons' Act, 1969 which provided for intermediate treatment for delinquent or pre-delinquent children, and later from the shift in policies and attitudes towards diverting children from institutions to family living and the need felt to prepare them for such a move. Unlike the earlier American examples, groups for children in care are now being used to prepare them before they move to new families or to independent living in the community, with only scanty examples of groups being used for purely therapeutic aims. It can be said that the concept of 'preparation' as an objective obscures ideas about therapy without diminishing them. Also, unlike the earlier examples, current groupwork in this area is much more structured and task orientated, combining discussion with activity rather than having discussion alone. In fact, activity sometimes predominates over discussion.

The activities, which include games, exercises and role-play, have been developed for the purpose or adapted from other fields (e.g. I.T. groups) because they are seen as relevant and appropriate for the task of preparation. The activities are structured in such a way as to promote purposeful interaction within the group, e.g. preparing posters about oneself, role-playing the introduction to a new family or playing a game. Besides their preparatory nature, activities can also give assessment clues which can be used when matching children and carers. Not surprisingly, perhaps, some groupworkers put more of the emphasis on activities whilst others try to keep a balance between 'talking about facts and feelings' and activities. If talking is associated with therapy, activities are seen as performing the dual function of putting children at ease and also facilitating interaction. Like Water- house's views on I.T. groups (1978) no clear distinction can be drawn between therapy and activity. He describes how I.T. groups were considerably influenced by ideas from the educational field, with some of the group leaders then and now having backgrounds in education. Ideas about the use of 'discussion, role play and games' which were a characteristic of the I.T. groups were transferred and adapted to preparatory groups for children before joining new families. Brown and Caddick (1986) view these developments as part of a 'British model' of groupwork which was practice-generated and 'emphasized agency function (Care and Control) as well as client need and worker values'.

The model that has emerged from the recent use of groups with children in care is of groups that are: purposeful, contractual, task-orientated, well-structured, combining activity and discussion around a separate theme or topic each time, and involving four to six children. A larger group, some practitioners argue, may impede the more individual attention required when games and exercises are introduced. Unlike some of the earlier American examples of separating the sexes there is now an explicit attempt to keep a balance between boys and girls. The groups meet either weekly or fortnightly over a period of about three months.

At the outset, the preparatory groups described here may appear too structured, with the group leader largely determining the process. It is still a matter for speculation whether the approach detracts from more free-flowing interaction and particularly the sharing of feelings such as anxieties or fears about the future. Obviously much can depend on how the activities are introduced and structured, leading to a more relaxed atmosphere promoting discussion. The danger of activities becoming ends in themselves is perhaps reduced by linking each activity to a specific purpose and by allowing time for reflection and feedback.

Leadership issues

The leader's role has to span both 'talking' and 'doing': he has to feel comfortable with both aspects. Besides an understanding of some universal group processes (e.g. leadership, dependency, task orientation and knowledge from the field of child care), leaders have also to make themselves acceptable to the group and make its members feel safe. Briscoe (1978), in her discussion of programme activities in social groupwork, identifies three main tools at the disposal of the worker to help the group achieve its purposes: his own skills at using himself to influence group interaction and the actions of the members; the interaction of the group itself and its impact on individual members; and the activity or programme content of the group or what the group actually does during the meetings.

Groups of the type described here require considerable advance planning and preparation by the group leaders, clarity about aims and close familiarity with activities and the purpose they can serve. Reference was also made to the need by the group workers to have knowledge and experience of child care work, i.e. adoption, foster care and residential work, because of the complexity entailed by such work which has to be reflected in the preparation. Furthermore, workers, particularly in multi-racial areas, need to have a good grasp of the impact of racism on black children and the need to safeguard and promote their cultural and racial awareness and identity.

Evaluation

Empirical evidence about the impact of preparatory work with children on an individual or group basis, before they move to new families or into the community, is again very limited. No study, so far as is known, has set out simply to evaluate the impact of such groups on subsequent adjustment and placement outcome. What we have is mostly indirect evidence from studies whose main focus was different. In addition, the idea of preparation being very recent, studies have not yet fully caught up with practice developments. What findings are available though, point unmistakably to the importance of preparatory work. For example, Kagan and Reid's (1986) study of emotionally disturbed youths placed for adoption, supports the need for a community service to be provided 'to youths' both before and after adoptive placement. Equally Berridge and Cleaver (1986) found from their study of foster placements that the preparation of the child was important for the stability of the fostering arrangement.

The contributors to this section

Pauline Hoggan describes the thinking behind, and gives examples of the use of groups for preparing young children to join permanent families. Sylvia Murphy and Marjorie Helm concentrate on adolescents who are being prepared to join foster families or community carers. Audrey Mullender, as already stated, describes how groupwork can be used to help black children placed transracially to develop their racial and cultural awareness.

7

Preparing children for family placement through the use of small groups

Pauline Hoggan

> No-one thought of giving explanations to small orphans,
> any more than to market-bound pigs
> Janet Hitchman, *The King of the Barbareens*)

INTRODUCTION

Hitchman's autobiography, from which the above quotation is taken, describes vividly what it is like to be a child in care being sent from pillar to post with no explanations and no power over one's life (the quotation was used effectively in the training pack produced by the Association of British Adoption and Fostering Agencies [ABAFA] in 1977). To me, and I am sure, to many other colleagues working primarily with children, it seems strange now to think of the effort and research work which had to be put into persuading child-care workers of how important it is to children to understand their current circumstances, their past relationships and what the future perhaps holds for them – and more important still, that such information, including participation in planning for their future, should be looked upon as a right to which children are entitled (see, for example, Triseliotis, 1973).

Mainly as a result of the challenge faced during the past decade to find families for older children, many agencies started to develop new approaches which took account of the above. The use of groups was one way of helping to put across some of the points made earlier. Though there were some previous examples of groupwork with children in care, what was new was the use of groups as a means of preparing children to move to new families. With this in mind, Lothian Region Homefinding Team embarked in the early 1980s on a programme of groupwork for such children. Initially, the groups were based on a model described by Sim and O'Hara (1982). Our ideas have developed since then as a result of experience, feedback from the children, from new families, the children's social workers and the writings of people such as Fahlberg (1981) and Jewett (1984).

Context of the groupwork programme

When we started the programme in 1982 nearly all the children waiting were over nine and had been referred to the Lothian Regional Resource Exchange for a permanent new family, preferably on an adoptive basis. At this time we were dealing with the 'backlog' of children who had been identified during the 1970s as having been 'warehoused' in care. Most of these children had grown up in institutional care and indeed that was their current environment. In contrast, the profile of the children involved in the groups now has changed significantly. Most of the children referred currently are in temporary foster placements and have had very unsettled and uncertain lives, but tend not to have been in care for continuous periods of more than a year, as was the case in the past. As a result the children's parents are often still around and tenuous or more meaningful bonds may be maintained. Many of the children have also been subjected to physical and/or sexual abuse, as well as to quite marked rejection from adults in their natural families. To put it crudely, whereas our first groups of 'institutionalized' children did not have a clue how most people in our society live or how relationships operate, our children now would tend to have very painful conscious memories of the rawness and ambivalence that family life can have. The children on referral to us at present are between 5 and 12. Usually adoption would be the intention for the children of about 10 and under, whereas the children over 10 would either have the kind of significant relationships or identity with their family of origin that would lead our agency to the view that adoption as a primary aim is not viable. We would therefore be looking for a committed family placement where the child could hopefully spend most of the rest of his/her childhood and young adulthood. As we have gained experience we have also become more confident in using groups to work with much younger children, i.e. from 4 to 7, whereas when we started we assumed that these children might not gain much from the concepts we were attempting to present. We have also found that children of so-called limited ability appear to have gained much from the sessions.

At the time the children are referred to the Resource Exchange and therefore 'started' with a group, we would expect that their own area team worker would have involved the individual child in the planning for their future and would probably have done substantial work with them on their own history, possibly using the life story book as a tool. However, we would also expect that because of the mayhem of the children's life up to this point, they will be in a state of confusion and low self-esteem.

Purpose of the groups

The aim of the groups is to provide information for children in care who are waiting to move into a new family, focusing particularly on why children come into care, what it is like for children to move into new families and how social workers find new families for children. The second main aim is to provide support for the children while they are waiting for a family, through a group process involving a few other children in the same situation, and by working with two of the specialist social workers who are most involved in finding and placing similar children in families. The groupwork programme provides workers in the Homefinding Team with an opportunity to meet and work with the children face to face. This is an invaluable part of the process of attempting to link up the children to 'the most appropriate family for them'. We also hope that the group sessions can provide opportunities and new openings for their own social workers to continue their work with the children. It is important to state that we see the groups as having a minor, not major, therapeutic effect in helping children resolve their feelings of distress. As our work in placing special needs children has developed and we realize the degree of pain which these children carry, we feel increasingly sceptical of the approach to this kind of work which seems to view a social worker as a magical medium who can spirit away all the pain of a child who has been abused and rejected. In the same vein we would clearly not use the group process as a reason for holding back a child for placement. Hopefully, the timing of the groups is regular and flexible enough for nearly all the children to participate, without interfering in the timing of their placement. We have to acknowledge that it is in placement that the real work of growth and attachment can begin, not at a time when feelings are blocked by uncertainty and anxiety about the past and future. Post-placement work is currently done on an individual basis, but we are hoping soon to experiment with the use of groups for some adopted young people.

The opportunity to meet with other children creates a deliberate focus, providing a degree of anonymity and often an alternative to the intense, one-to-one approach. As the areas dealt with in the groups are extremely painful for the children, they are often unlikely to be able to cope intellectually or emotionally with direct questioning. By using more indirect methods, like games, quizzes and role-play, it is possible to create a more relaxed environment in which the children may express themselves to a greater and deeper extent. In such a situation the children often 'trigger off' thoughts and feelings in each other which are followed by involved conversations about difficult areas of their lives. We often find that the children are able to test out their own thoughts and fantasies with their peers and raise issues which they might be afraid to mention in one-to-one sessions. The workers and other children provide both factual information and examples of how things really are and act as a sounding board for the other group members. This usually helps the children to clarify their values and begin to establish which of their thoughts and feelings are based on reality and which are rooted in fantasy. If a child decides, when things are getting too painful, to opt out of the group process just described, he may still take in what the other children and workers are discussing and can then raise these issues either in later group sessions or with an individual worker or carer, or perhaps later on with a trusted new parent.

Working with the child in a group, as well as in an individual setting, provides a valuable insight into how the child might relate to others. In addition, it is possible to both observe and experience the child interacting with peers and adults. This helps the worker to build up a more vivid and realistic picture of the child, which can then be passed on to potential adopters. However, we try to use observations from group interactions as guidelines, rather than as 'tablets of stone', in subsequent decision-making.

Logistics

There are usually three to four children in each group, with two leaders who are social workers in the Homefinding Team, which has six workers in all. We have had groups with more children but have found with higher numbers, e.g. a group of three lots of siblings, that the children can miss out on a degree of intimacy and one-to-one contact. We nearly always hold the groups in our Homefinding Room where posters made by the children waiting for families are displayed, including posters of children who are now placed with new families. Not surprisingly perhaps, in a reasonably compact area like Lothian Region with approximately 800,000 population, there is a grapevine among children in care and often those who attend the groups will recognize photos of one of the other children through schools, shared foster placements, etc.

Timing

There are usually four sessions, held once a week for four weeks. We have found the best time to be in the afternoon. Obtaining time off school for the children has not been a problem as the sessions have been regarded in the same way as hospital and other important appointments. This also marks the group's significance to the children, i.e. it is not a leisure activity. It also means that the children are not tired after a full day at school and that we do not incur the same transport difficulties as there can be when overtime is involved. Either the child's social worker or foster parents usually take the children to and from the group. The group can be set in length at between an hour and an hour and a half. Some workers feel that an hour can be too rushed, whereas an hour and a half can feel as if it is straining the concentration of the children.

The contract

The motivation of the children involved is usually very high but it is essential that the adults involved acknowledge to each other and to the children, where appropriate, the fear and anxiety that is present in them. As well as nervousness to do with starting an event like the group, in the foreground for all the children is the total uncertainty of their lives. Experience suggests that in their minds must be questions such as – 'Is it my fault I am in care?'; 'Will anybody want me?'; 'What will they be like, will they batter me?' In preparing for the group, the Homefinding Team workers will at least have had some basic information about the children following their referal to the Lothian Resource Exchange. One of the Homefinding Team workers will have been present at the Adoption Panel discussion which registered the child as needing a new family and the workers will, of course, have access to the child's background. Understandably, when a group is in preparation the social workers and carers may be concerned about the children's potential behaviour at the group or the kind of revelations they may make there. It is important for them and for the children to allay fantasies about what we will be expecting the children to do. Letters are sent out to the workers and carers of the children involved, inviting the child to the group and the adults concerned to a pre-group meeting. A provisional plan of the programme is also sent out. The pre-group meeting is attended by the group leaders, the children's workers and the carers. At this meeting, which usually lasts about an hour, and takes place in the Homefinding Room where the groups will meet, we ask the adults involved with the children to bring us up to date on the situation and to highlight concerns they may have about them, or about the children's presence at the group. For example, carers may worry that the children will not be able to manage written work or will find it distressing to talk about being in care. We explain the purpose of the group clearly and set out the contract on practicalities and expectations, e.g. that we won't see it as a negative reflection on the foster parents if the child is badly behaved but rather as a reaction to the stress involved or a behavioural pattern. We make a commitment to recording each session and to sharing this with the workers and carers and also invite them to a post-group meeting when we will discuss the group and return any material the children have prepared. We will also have prepared a letter to the child inviting him or her to the group and will ask one of the adults to pass it on to the child as part of their own discussions with him/her about the sessions.

Themes and contents of session

We tend to use the same basic themes in each set of sessions, but feel free to be flexible and adapt methods as new ideas emerge and also in accordance with the age, ability and needs of different children. It is useful for the workers involved to have some knowledge of children's games, interests and current fashions. As well as using one's own imagination there are now a range of books, articles and resources to provide ideas on how to run groups effectively (e.g. British Agencies for Adoption and Fostering (BAAF) Publications). However, it is important to remember that activities such as games, written work and role-plays are tools to assist and facilitate communication within the group, and that the task of the group is not to get through the detailed programme which one has set out, at the expense of being insensitive to lines for discussion which may be presented by the children. Workers use of their own experience of life and its ups and downs can be used effectively when a child has managed to say something small but valid about a feeling such as sadness. At the start of each session we explain to the children why we are holding the group and what the theme for the week is. Usually we plan two or three exercises and discussions and some unwinding time. We also try to have a balance of active group exercises and individual writing and drawing work. Having this kind of balance can dispel any impression the children may have that they are being pressured into discussion of feelings all the time. A typical group sequence aims to work around the following topics:

Who I am and why I'm here
How we find families
What families get to know about us
What is it going to be like in a new family

Session one: 'Who I am and why I'm here'
When the children arrive with their social worker or carer they are always feeling anxious, usually showing visible signs of nervousness, such as paleness or jumpiness. At the start they often become involved in studying the posters on the wall, asking what has happened to particular children. Most of this session consists of fairly superficial getting-to-know-you types of games to help the children warm up and relax. We usually start with an icebreaker game such as throwing a ball or furry rabbit round in a circle and shouting the name of the person to whom one is throwing it, or each person who gets the ball or the rabbit shouting his/her name. Then perhaps we suggest that a good way to get to know each other is by asking questions as the TV interviewers do. The leader shows the children cards which have questions such as 'what is your age?', 'what is your favourite TV programme?', 'which school are you attending?', 'who is your favourite pop star?' and then shows the children how they would go about interviewing each other using as props a cardboard TV and mikes. The children are usually slow to begin with and can be very quiet and uncertain about what they are supposed to do. With a little encouragement they usually begin asking questions of each other and of the leader and get into the spirit of the

game. I noted after one session that 'the two little ones needed more help with reading the questions and J, in particular, was still speaking almost inaudibly'. Old telephones can also be used in the same way to conduct interviews of this kind.

We usually spend the rest of the structured part of the session starting the children off on their individual life-maps, based on Fahlberg's 'eco-maps' (1981, p. 39). We explain that these will be a bit like their individual posters but are related more to what has happened to them in the past and what they want in the future. We emphasize that the posters are for themselves and that at the end of the sessions we will give them to their social workers or carer to pass back to them. We explain also that each week we will be asking them to add different things. During the first session we ask them to start off with a drawing of the house they live in now and either a list or drawings of the people who live with them. If there is time they can go on to do perhaps their school and teacher or their social worker and what his or her job is for them.

At the end of the work, juice and crisps are passed round. We usually work out a rota of who should have first choice. By the end of the group the children seem keen to return. One group of children, who were meeting before Christmas, suggested spending some time at one session making Christmas decorations so that they could decorate the Homefinding Room for us. In my notes on M (aged 7), I commented that he seemed 'to identify his present foster family very much as his family and was perhaps less aware than P, his older sister, of the uncertainty of his situation'. On T, I wrote: 'The first thing T wrote after her name on the life-map was that she had "good foster parents". I got the impression that she is feeling very conscious about having to be good and acceptable at the moment.' 'S was very quiet and pale at the start of the group. When asked things, he would take a long time to reply but then would answer thoughtfully. He was the slowest at working on his life-map and quite a perfectionist but he certainly was concentrating on what he was doing . . . he quietly mentioned to one of us that he might get to play for the school football team, which seemed very important to him.'

Session two: 'How we find families'
We have learned that children can have some very strange ideas about how families are found. A game is introduced called 'Find a Family' which is used to stimulate discussion about where new families come

105

from. It is a kind of true-false quiz. It involves a pack of cards with serious and light-hearted suggestions about how families are found, such as 'we advertize on TV or in newspapers?', or 'E.T. brings families to us?', or 'we put up posters in post offices?', or 'we drag them out of pubs?' The children have to decide which cards are jokes and which are realistic. They usually debate between them which are right and which are wrong. Not surprisingly perhaps, some children may start to argue, giggle or lose concentration.

Another activity is the 'Happy Families' card game. During one session when this game was played, S commented dryly 'what if it was as easy in real life to get a family?' L also pointed out that the card game families all had a mum, dad, sister and brother which wasn't necessarily the composition of all families. S said that wasn't what her family had been like, and the others went on to say what kind of family they had or were in just now. We often use this game to promote discussion on the possibility of going to a single parent family.

During this session more work is done on the life-maps and the children put answers to more difficult questions such as: 'the best thing that happened this year', or 'what I dream about'. Answers to 'what I dream about' have included 'a new family', 'ghosts and monsters', or 'having drugs pushed on me'. Comments to the question 'what I worry about' have included 'moving to another family, or moving schools'. I noted S's head-twitching briefly recurred while she was talking about the C family within which she had been placed with a view to adoption but where it hadn't worked out.

We may go on to play 'Family Jigsaw'. This is a game designed to get the children to think about what kind of a family they might like to live with. They are asked to choose pieces of the jigsaw puzzle which we made up from magazine photos of families, and told that while they put the pieces in the different puzzles, they should try and think hard about how they would fit in, if they were a piece of jigsaw. The game helps many children become involved. Subjects raised include: families with cars, families with grannies, single parents, brothers and sisters, houses with gardens, small families and big families. In one group a girl wanted a mum and dad with no children to take her and her little brother. K was not keen on a girl the same age as herself and referred to her unhappy fostering experience with a single woman. On the whole she would prefer two parents. The discussion is then broadened to what the children thought it was most important we should find out about families. S said that she would find out if they were 'suitable' and if they really wanted children who weren't their own. I noted later, 'S seems to be very ready for another placement and she can express her feelings of fear for the future. She is a socially able and very attractive girl . . .' 'M was competitive for attention. She was showing off her book of photos of her old family to the others. The group seems to be raising important issues for K and he has mentioned his brothers a few times.'

By the end of the second session, I noted, the children forge some kind of bond in recognizing that they are all in the same boat and begin to offer some support to each other, e.g. 'K and M encouraged S to come to the Adoption Club with them. The theme on 'how we find families' seems to concentrate their attention.'

Session three: 'What families get to know about us'
This session usually begins with a 'Follow my Leader' game which introduces the idea of how children need to learn the rules of new families and how difficult it is to enter other families' explicit or covert rules. The game is played with the children taking turns to lead the rest of the group (including the leader) round the room, at the same time making rules which the others have to follow. This game also helps to make the point that family life is complex and that like a game whose rules you do not know, it takes time watching before you can work them out. 'Twister', the commercial game, is another activity which helps to put across the idea both of complexity and of trying to enter or understand the rules of a new family without knowing the background and context within which family dynamics were developed. We have found that some children go to families that have strict rules about such things as watching TV or going to bed, whilst others go to families who are more flexible or entirely *laissez-faire*. One child who had been rejected by his long-term foster parents, without understanding the reason, remarked: 'All families have rules, it's just that they're harder to find in some than others.'

The so-called 'Habits' game involves children taking turns to pick a card, each card showing a habit or way of behaving. Discussion then follows on how the children feel about it or whether they would like it or not. This game helps get over the idea that new families can know that children may come to them with certain habits, problems and feelings. For example, in one of the groups, T got a card which said 'sometimes I spoil things for other people.' Her head immediately went down as if she had been quite used in the past to being automatically criticized and undermined. In the end she was able to say quite timidly that she did not think she did spoil things for others and we warmly backed this up as this had not been our experience of her in the group. At this her face lit up. S got a card which said 'I like to forget about the past.' The children remarked that you couldn't really do that even though there were things you would want to forget if you could. P got a card saying 'I wet my bed': she said she didn't, but her little brother got very excited and made a fuss saying that she did. P was most irate at this. We then tried to give an example of how you could wet the bed when you were really anxious about something. M got a card saying: 'I lose my temper' which gave P a chance to get back at him! J got a card which said 'sometimes I am moody and huffy' but he said he behaves like this only when somebody hits him, and denied that he does anything to provoke it. When one of them got a card saying 'I like to be cuddled' three others said openly that they liked that too. C's card said 'I sometimes steal.' At this he said 'No', but looked very directly at D who looked sheepish and then admitted he sometimes pinches C's sweets.

Other statements on the cards include: 'I sometimes cry in bed', 'I sometimes hit out at people', 'I dirty my pants', 'I cannot make friends', 'I like my own way', 'I sometimes lose my temper', 'Occasionally I tell lies', 'Sometimes I feel lonely', 'I find it difficult to say what I feel', and 'I like to be tucked up in bed at night'. When we first tried this game we were criticized for using such an intense game with the children, but interestingly, it was the game which the children opted to do again when they had some spare time in the last session.

Towards the end of the session the children have time again to continue with their life-maps: 'C drew his school and a sign to the school correctly spelt! He wrote that he liked sums but could not think of what he did not like, so having written "I hate . . .", completed it by putting "going to school". I noted later that during this meeting, 'P kept flitting about from one thing to another but she can respond to keeping to one thing when an adult pay hers enough attention. P is both anxious to please whilst also looking for praise. T also enjoys praise but she never becomes attention seeking in an over-anxious way. On the other hand J seemed to want to disrupt the group with his behaviour. For example, he paired with M and was involved with him in interrupting things. This was possibly not unrelated to the anxiety raised by the topics under discussion.'

Session four: 'What is it going to be like in a new family?'
This session starts with a game based on imagining the children had just been told that a family had been found for them. In answer to the question of what they would say on first meeting their new family, C (aged 12) said 'Hello' (his new family would consist of a mum and dad) and that his own feelings would be 'What is it going to be like?' J (aged 10) would say 'Hello mummy, I will be adopted by you' and added that he thought the first meeting 'could be in a house' and that there would be 'my mum and dad and a dog and a girl'. C (aged 12) would say 'I was happy and glad' and that the family would remark 'Hello, where did you come from?' 'What school did you go to?' and, 'Do you like watching TV?'; he wrote down 'When I went to meet a new family I felt happy and nervous'.

Another exercise involves cards with a 'feeling' adjective written on each of the cards. Each child is then asked to choose all those cards describing their feelings about going to a new family. The cards cover such feelings as: 'happy', 'empty', 'helpful', 'glad', 'excited', 'brave', 'calm', 'nervous', 'sad' and 'strange'. For R the key word was to be 'excited' as this seemed to reflect her feelings at the prospect of a move. We got the impression that she has high hopes of her new family. She seemed more suspended in limbo than the others in the group and her expectations of a family seemed unreal. When asked to choose a feeling the family might have, she picked 'jealousy'. This generated discussion between the children as to whether they would be treated equally with the family's own children. G (aged 8) said 'you would need to be brave to move', but he then substituted this with 'surprise' at getting a family. He chose 'wonderful' as a feeling the family would have and explained that this was because they might not have any children and therefore would be glad to have him. C was very honest about his feelings, saying he thought he would be 'nervous' when first meeting a new family. Also that he would feel 'strange' at first as he had done for the first couple of days in his foster home. The choice of 'sad' related to his feelings about leaving his foster family. He seemed realistic but not unduly worried about such a move.

As in previous sessions, the children spent time working on their life-maps. R was asked to draw a picture of what she thought her new home would be like and drew a house in the country because she had never lived there before. She would also share a room with the daughter of the house, and there definitely had to be a dog in the house. When linking the new house to others where she had been before, she listed two Children's Homes, her mother's home and 'lots of foster parents'. S listed in his previous life all four of his little brothers, who were now split with 'relatives and another family. He was able to describe all their looks and personalities vividly to me. When I commented that he must be very sad about the split, he commented that he was, but the most important thing now was that he and D stayed together and found a mum and dad.'

At the end of the fourth session, the children usually show a marked reluctance to leave and indeed our only real reason for not continuing the groups during the children's waiting time is pressure of work and time on us, the adults. We occasionally have an 'Adoption Club Outing' for the children waiting and aim to have a waiting support group for those children, usually over 10, who linger on referral.

Post-group meeting

We discuss the groups with the childrens' workers and carers, and hear how the children have reacted. Some children describe the groups in great detail to their carers or pursue this with their social worker, but many keep it private. For some children the groups have sparked off a period of testing out behaviour and it is important for the professionals to be ready to use this constructively and not push the feelings aroused underground. Sometimes the post-group meeting can clarify the future work or planning for a child further, e.g. one foster parent commented that the groups had reinforced for her areas that she would have to highlight even more in her preparation work with the child, even though she had thought she was doing this adequately.

It is of course important for the leaders to build in time to record the sessions and have these passed on to the workers and carers. As we have had video equipment available to us recently, it has been tempting to film the groups. However, we acknowledge that this would affect the dynamics and privacy of the sessions and perhaps filming should only be used as an activity in itself, e.g. the children using the mike and camera as an interviewing game.

Looking back

We have now run groups for over 100 children on referral to the Lothian Resource Exchange. The salient lesson for us as workers has been to learn to respect the children's resilience and commitment to the future despite their hitherto depressing experiences. In this context we must be careful, in building on their hopes, not to promote unrealistic expectations that we are fairy godmothers who are waving the magic wand of adoption as the solution to their pain. Given half a chance, many of the children are able to engage in a realistic level of discussion about the difficulties in adjusting to the new situation of placement for adoption, where the stakes are very high for them. Indeed one girl who had been labelled as almost illiterate was able to pick out, without hesitation, cards displaying multi-syllabled words such as 'distraught', 'betrayed' and 'devastated' because these were feelings that as a 12-year-old she had experienced to a degree unknown to us, the worldly wise adults!

Although I have described a structure we have developed for running our groupwork programme, the suggestions we have for specific activities should be primarily regarded as a context in which to promote communication and acknowledgement of feelings. In our experience, the most useful resource which workers can develop for the programme are the courage and confidence to elicit and accept the children's pain.

Note: The material for this chapter is drawn from the work of the children referred to Lothian Regional Resource Exchange between 1982–6, the staff of the Homefinding Team and David Shipman, a former student with the Unit.

8

Group preparation of adolescents for family placement

Sylvia Murphy and Marjorie Helm

THE FAMILY PLACEMENT PROJECT

Barnardo's Family Placement Project (N. East Division) was set up in 1980 to offer planned, family-based care for teenagers (14 plus) on a time-limited basis. One of the primary aims of the project was to increase the range of options for teenagers in care as it was recognized at the time that there was a dearth of this type of provision. The team currently comprises one project leader, four full-time and two part-time social workers.

Each placement is made with explicit aims negotiated during the introductory period and agreed at the Placement Meeting. Provisional time-limits are also agreed, some placements being negotiated in six-month blocks. The project is based on the belief that given training and support, families can provide appropriate care and control for many teenagers who have experienced difficulties both in their own families and in residential care. Teenagers placed with the project retain the involvement and support of their own local authority social workers. Project staff, it was envisaged, would be primarily involved in the recruitment, assessment, training and support of foster families. A course of training sessions based on the NFCA's 'Added to Adolescent/ Parenting Plus' package is initially offered to foster parents before they join one of the support groups. There is a recognition within the project of the value of the mutual support between foster parents which is generated by this type of group. Gradually, however, members of the project team became aware of the disparity between input into preparation of foster parents as opposed to foster teenagers, a point which also emerged from Shaw and Hipgrave's study (1983). There was recognition of the lower levels of preparatory work being undertaken with teenagers prior to going into placement and the need to expand this form of work. The aim now is to offer the opportunity of attending a preparation group to all teenagers referred to the project.

Target group

The group was aimed at teenagers, both male and female, aged 14 to 18 years old, referred for family placement by Social Service Departments. The only selection criteria for inclusion in the group were the absence of incapacitating anxiety, and a certain level of literacy. It was also the initial intention to avoid having too many youngsters who tended to be withdrawn or who might 'act out' or be intellectually too limited. This, however, had to be abandoned because the information given by agencies at the referral stage could not reliably be used to predict the youngsters' behaviour in the group. Our experience now is that it is difficult to absorb more than 2 to 3 teenagers who require a great deal of help in expressing themselves verbally or participating in tasks. It is also important to have a reasonable balance of girls and boys within the group.

Aims, objectives and principles

The overall aim of providing such a group was to achieve more successful family placements. As previously noted, the teenagers were at vastly different stages of preparedness in terms of their understanding of family life and family placement and their commitment or otherwise to such a placement. We saw thorough preparation of a teenager as essential if placements were to have any chance of being successful. We always envisaged our group as supplementing, and not replacing, individual work being undertaken with the teenager.

Besides the opportunity afforded to group members to share experiences, another objective was to increase the teenagers' understanding of their present situation and boost their self-image. It was also hoped that the group would give the teenagers more realistic expectations of family life so that they could make a more informed choice as to: (a) whether they wanted a family placement, and (b) if so, what sort of family they wanted. Top priority was to involve the teenagers as fully as possible in decision-making and, as well, to give them an enjoyable experience.

It was envisaged originally that all participants in the group would attend prior to being placed with a family. In practice this has not proven to be the case. Again because of relatively small numbers we often had to delay the start of the group in order to reach the required membership. This inevitably meant that some teenagers had already been introduced to a family and, in a few cases, had been placed. Far from this proving problematic, it turned out to be a positive advantage as these first-hand experiences were shared with other group members. It is important, however, to maintain a balanced membership to avoid a situation where one or two members are left without any potential family in view.

Initial preparations

The co-leaders of each group began by having a frank discussion about their individual styles of leadership, their strengths and weaknesses as perceived by themselves and each other, in order to assess their ability to work together. The discussions also resolved basic issues like size of group, number of sessions, venue, people to inform, method of supervision and evaluation.

In terms of giving the teenagers a more realistic idea of family placement we realized we could not launch into an exploration of 'new' families without paying some attention to past experiences. In other words, we needed to look back somewhat before looking forward. This could only be covered in a fairly superficial way as the group was obviously not the place to undertake 'life story' work (ideally this kind of work should already have been done although sadly this was often not the case). Our main purpose was to help group members give some thought to how they arrived at their present situation. At the time that individual teenagers are referred to the Project, we mention the preparation group to their workers who in turn talk to the teenagers about it. Once dates are finalized, a meeting is held at the office for the field and residential social workers responsible for the care of potential group members to discuss the group and stimulate enthusiasm. On completion of the group sessions a further meeting is held to give feedback to them.

Following the initial meeting with the social workers, the co-leaders visit each prospective group member individually in order to secure their agreement to attend the group. The basic rules of the group are explained and practical details given in addition to some idea of the content. Each group member is asked to agree that they: (i) would help each other; (ii) would not be verbally abusive to each other; and (iii) would not physically abuse each other. There has never been any violence in the group, but it has been felt necessary to set limits at the outset. It is also explained to potential members that what they say during group sessions will remain confidential to the group and will not be reported back to their workers. The only exception would be in the unlikely event of a member sharing some information that, because of its importance and seriousness, had to be passed on. In such an eventuality the matter would be discussed with that member after the session had ended to secure his/her agreement.

Content and methods

We have chosen to discuss the content, process and specific methods used in the various sessions in four sections or stages of the group: Forming (Sessions One and Two), Storming (Session Three), Norming and Performing (Sessions Four, Five and Six) and Ending (Session Seven). (See Tuckman 1965.)

The groups described here were run over a period of three years from October 1983 to the present time and ranged in numbers between five and nine. Inevitably, the composition of the different groups affected their functioning and the focus of individual sessions, something that will be referred to when describing the activities of the group.

Forming (Sessions One and Two): Relationships and interactions

The majority of young people coming to the groups are strangers to one another, some coming from quite long distances and carrying a high level of anxiety and uncertainty. For some it will be their first experience of being part of a group. This kind of anxiety is also manifest in the relatively formal relationships which are usually established in the early stages of the group; invariably, boys and girls' sub-groupings are the most frequent. By the end of Session two there is evidence of the beginning of alliances within the group and also of a protectiveness to the most vulnerable members. In one group two of the girls took the most anxious member under their wing and in another, one of the more socially-skilled girls adopted a protective role towards two other less-skilled girls. Understandably at this stage interactions are fairly guarded with none of the group members willing to expose themselves very much.

The activities have as their theme 'getting to know one another' and include a variety of games and exercises intended to reduce anxiety, facilitate co-operation and find common ground. We begin to look in very general terms at the differences between residential care and family life and, finally, draw up an agreed statement of the aims of the group.

Session One: The first session starts with a variety of ice-breakers, one of which is the 'Ball Game' where a ball is thrown between members who firstly shout out their own names, then the name of the person to whom they are throwing it and finally the name of the person who has thrown the ball to them. This is followed by rounds of 'I like' and 'I don't like' and the Word Association Game which involves guessing words written on cards from clues given by the card-holder. In the second half of the session, members begin to share basic information about themselves such as: where we live now, something we like about it and something we don't like and where we would ideally like to live. This leads into a discussion as to the relative advantages and disadvantages of living in families as opposed to living in a residential situation. The group winds up by drawing up some objectives which members hope to achieve during the life of the group.

The objectives of this particular session are to introduce group members to one another and begin the process of developing some group cohesion, by a gradual sharing of information about one another and setting goals for joint working. The following thoughts and feelings expressed by one group member are typical, we suspect, of those of other young people coming to the group for the first time: 'My first experience of the group was that I was very nervous and kept thinking; Would they find a family for me? How long would I have to wait? What would the different families be like? Gradually we all became much more relaxed and I found that I enjoyed the games, much to my surprise . . .'

Session Two: The theme of this session is trust. By acknowledging that many of the group members will have experienced being 'let down' in the past, group members are encouraged to share both positive and negative feelings about families and the idea of fostering. This can be helpful not only to those who felt let down, but also to other members in the group.

A game which has proved popular and which was originally used so that one boy in a wheelchair could participate is called 'blindfold leading'. This involves group members pairing off with a member of the group with whom they have not been acquainted prior to attending the group. One of the pair puts on a blindfold and, as far as possible, entrusts himself to his partner who then leads him around a prescribed area (usually the ground floor of the office building); the roles are then reversed. One of the group members commented about this session: 'I remember it was hard to have complete confidence in someone who you hardly knew to lead you blindfold around a room; and I also remember feeling quite scared at the same time and not quite sure what I had let myself in for.'

Next follows a discussion about trust – about the feeling of being let down or having a trust betrayed – and again we refer to the confidentiality of issues discussed within the group. Latterly, we have introduced this by a number of brief role plays given by group leaders of situations with which a teenager can readily identify where a trust has been broken. This has facilitated discussion and provided an introduction to the idea of role play in which it is hoped the group members will share at the later stages. Though this discussion can prove quite painful for some of the young people, we have been struck by the fact that, if a number of members are willing to share their feelings at this stage, it can greatly enhance the cohesion of the group. For example, in one group two members were able to identify with feelings of having been let down and disappointed by their families, and by previous attempts to find them foster parents which had failed despite advertisements, etc.

An attempt is then made to lighten the atmosphere of the group by a game called 'Pass the Squeeze' where members hold hands in a circle with one person in the centre. One of the leaders starts off the game by squeezing the hand of the person on his right, for example, who then squeezes the hand of the person on his right and so on. The person in the centre of the circle closes his eyes for a few seconds and then has to try and locate the squeeze. Having done so, he then changes place with the person he has caught 'passing the squeeze'. This game also provides an opportunity for physical contact between group members.

The session is rounded off with a couple of written exercises to give a change of activity, particularly for those who feel more comfortable writing than talking. These involve completing a list of sentences beginning:

I want . . . . I like . . . . I'm afraid of . . . . I need . . . . I hate . . . .
I laugh at . . . .

Members are also asked to complete a personal shield with such headings as: My Biggest Success/My Biggest Failure of the Year/My Hope for Next Year/My Hope for Five Years from Now, etc.

GROUPWORK IN ADOPTION AND FOSTER CARE

Again, members are encouraged to share their written work if they want to, thus building up the sharing of information and trust within the group. The session ends on a light-hearted note with a group tangle in which members and leaders all join hands and then proceed to wind around or weave in and out of one another until they are in a 'tangle' whereupon they must 'unwind', still holding hands, which again involves light-hearted physical contact.

Storming (Session Three)

This session involves looking back in order eventually to move forward. We recognize that before asking the group members to consider their future plans, there has to be some acknowledgement of the significant and sometimes painful events of their past life. Again, this may create opportunities to establish links between one another as common factors emerge which we hope may help them to feel less 'isolated' and 'different'. It is also a session where they are encouraged to think in more positive terms about themselves and other group members. The assumption is that encouraging them to share and listen to one another's information can lead to a greater valuing of self and one another. From looking at self, members move on gradually to consider families in more depth and some of the process can again be experienced as quite painful.

The group members, by this stage, are feeling more confident and appear more lively and less compliant than previously. There is on the whole, however, a gradual increase in the range and number of interactions between group members and alliances forming between sub-groups. The internal disruption of the group varies. On one occasion, for example, the temporary absence of the boy who had emerged as the leader of the group led to much rivalry and disruption amongst the other boys vying for his position.

Techniques for this session have changed probably more than in any other. The session usually begins with a game called 'In Common' which involves moving around to sit next to someone with whom you have something 'in common', e.g. dress, hobbies, etc. This exercise is meant to build on the sharing of previous weeks and to develop further links between various group members. The exercise may result in two members pairing up because they are both wearing blue jeans or enjoy football or ice-skating. Others may pair when they discover that they have both lived in the same children's home or assessment centre at some time in their past or because they both find going to school difficult.

In one group we tackled the subject of 'coming into care' by undertaking a role-play of a young person being admitted to care for non-school attendance. Interestingly, one group member created a role for herself as an Educational Welfare Officer, which she found a novel experience as she herself had been truanting prior to coming into care. She later wrote of this session: 'In other sessions we did role-plays . . . trouble with a child who was constantly playing truant and behaving badly to his mother/father. At first it was hard to put yourself into a particular role and even harder coping with a bad-tempered father who wasn't going to listen to you or a child who was being very obnoxious towards you.'

In one of the other groups we were aware that the role-play might generate considerable anxiety, so we developed the idea of drawing out a 'Roadway Life Map', marking significant events on it, and then encouraging those willing to do so to share theirs with the group.

An alternative role-play tried in another group was that of a social worker discussing fostering with a teenager in residential care. This was only moderately successful and indicated to us the necessity of giving time to prepare for role-play and to get into role. In a more recent group this exercise was repeated, now using the gradual participation of one of the group members in the role-play. This was so successful that members insisted on the remainder of the session being given over to a role-play of a Planning Meeting! Another activity tried with more recent groups has been the use of talk-cards in which the youngster is asked to complete a sentence such as: 'I get angry when . . .' or 'When I have spare time I like to . . .'. At different times we have also made use of written exercises such as Family Crests and Personal Shields.

Norming and Performing (Sessions Four, Five and Six)

At this stage each of the groups have been at their most cohesive and group members have been able to concentrate on the tasks assigned to them. The tasks relate specifically to families. In Session Four the group settles down to consider the reality of families which we then build on for Session Five.

In each group we have used a 'brainstorm' to focus thinking on the subject of families. This has proved to be a productive method of opening up the topic. Group members are asked to shout out words/phrases that come to mind when thinking about families. One of the group leaders writes up these responses on a flip chart in the form of a list without discussing each one. The object of this exercise is to stimulate group members' thinking about families and what a family means to them. It is also a way of helping them to get into the next activity, namely the family collage. In addition, the group leaders are able to gain some useful information which could be examined in greater detail later on. In the 'brainstorm' about families we expected quite a lot of material suggestions, e.g. video, cars, TV, holidays, etc. but in fact we were often presented with many more intangibles such as: trust, love, the same people, people with time to spend with you. The activity that follows allows group members to indulge some of their fantasies, if they wish, by creating a collage of their ideal family. With one exception, in a recent group, this has proved to be a very popular and enjoyable activity for group members. The main purposes of it are:

(a) to encourage group members to continue to think about their own needs in terms of a family placement; and

(b) to provide a vehicle for all their ideas, whether rooted in reality or fantasy, before examining seriously their priorities in a more realistic manner.

In fact, most group members have thoughts about the characteristics they are looking for in foster parents as well as the more practical aspects.

In the fifth session we encourage some discussion of fears that group members might have in terms of the worst that could happen in a family. In some groups the teenagers were not very forthcoming but, in another, they raised several issues. Common to all groups, including more recent ones, is the fear of a rejection by foster parents. The reluctance of some members to consider such possibilities is not surprising, but we feel it is important to include this item. The next activity has proved to be popular and useful in stimulating ideas. A pile of cards is placed facing down, each with words written on that relate to living in a family, e.g., 'bed times', 'pocket money'. Each teenager is encouraged to highlight different attitudes and expectations. All members seem to enjoy this 'game' and are eager to take their turn.

The second half of the meeting consists of a question and answer session with two foster parents. The previous activity usually ensures no shortage of questions from group members. To meet with foster parents gives an example of at least one family's way of operating, and the questioning is often a two-way process. The material in this fifth session has been altered very little from the original planning because it has always worked well.

In the sixth session we begin to consider the introduction of a teenager to a family. In the form of a 'brainstorm', group members are asked to consider what information they need to know about a family before a first meeting and, conversely, what they think a family needs to know about them. Ideas are always forthcoming. In the second and third groups, two teenagers already in placement were invited to share their experience in terms of their introduction. This was not repeated in subsequent groups as we are still undecided about its potential usefulness. By this stage in its life the group has become very cohesive and members are reluctant to admit outsiders, at least those from their peer group.

Group members are encouraged at this session to think about the first meeting with foster parents in order to prepare them to take part in a role-play. They are then asked to role play a first meeting between one of them and a foster family. The idea is introduced before the break and roles are allocated in order to give some time for preparation. The 'foster home' scene is played out in our meeting room. Some teenagers choose their role, others ask to be allocated one. Group leaders are careful to match the role to the individual: for example, those who are very anxious or quiet are not given leading roles. There are usually a foster mother, foster father and several children in the family plus a social worker, a teenager and possibly a residential worker. The teenagers are asked to do all the wrong things initially which usually helps to dispel any tension and helps them into role. Many useful points can be drawn out before the second role-play, when we ask group members to replay the scene in the way they feel it should progress. Time is allowed for feedback from each individual. The success of this exercise has amazed us. It has also proved possible to include more withdrawn teenagers by allocating roles that demand little of them. Most role plays are recorded on video and most group members really enjoy the playback, as is indicated by the following comments: 'The videos were of a first meeting with foster parents going wrong. This was mainly because the foster parents weren't interested in the child. A successful meeting was also recorded. It was one big laugh all the way through and we also got our point across. It was funny seeing yourself on video at all angles. I was so different to what I expected myself to be.'

Endings (Session Seven)

In the final session an attempt is made to draw together the previous sessions and wind up the group. The task is somewhat lightened by the fact that the session is followed by an outing, a purely social event which is offered as a reward for all the effort the group members have made over the previous seven sessions. The organization of this outing would, if it were allowed to, absorb the whole of Session Seven. However, other activities are also squeezed in.

Feelings at this stage of the group are tinged both with relief and regret on the part of the leaders as well as the participants. There is a sense in which members anticipate the ending of the group and begin to draw apart. Preoccupations from outside impinge more noticeably on the group, particularly for those young people who are coming to the conclusion that fostering is not an option for them.

This session is essentially one of consolidation and so a considerable amount of time is given over to recapping on previous sessions and on technicalities. There is also some input on Placement Agreement and Placement Meetings as these help to make our type of family placements different from conventional fostering. (Placement meetings are convened before a young person joins a family and are used mainly to draw up an agreement between the different parties. Participants may include: the foster parents, the child's social worker, the residential social worker, the project social worker, the child and, if available, the parents.) The discussion is often somewhat stilted and it is debateable, as mentioned above, as to whether such an important topic should be left until the last session. In a recent group, where the members responded much better to games and role playing than to group discussion, we used the game 'True or False' to establish facts or dispel myths about Placement Meetings.

In addition, we complete another shield to compare with the one from Session Two and ask group members to fill out an evaluation questionnaire as well as watching a replay of previous videos. One teenager observed that discussion of Placement Meetings had made him feel better about his own imminent one, particularly the contribution made by one of the other members who had already had her meeting.

Some leadership issues

The leadership style is set before the group sessions commence, when the leaders visit the teenagers in their residential units. It is explained to them individually that the group will be run on very structured lines. We feel that this prior contact with the group leaders plus the security of a fairly tight structure helps to relieve some of the anxieties, particularly of the first two sessions.

The leadership tasks in terms of keeping the group to the planned agenda, controlling and nurturing the group, are shared equally between the group leader and co-leader throughout all the sessions. With a few exceptions in Sessions One and Two there is relatively little challenge to the leadership, most members being compliant. The third session is usually very hard work, principally to hold group members to the tasks. There have been attempts to challenge the leadership but no really serious threat has emerged. It has usually been possible to make some progress in this session. Most of the work of the group takes place in Sessions Four, Five and Six as group members seem most able to concentrate by now. In each group it has been noticeable that members have taken on the responsibility for controlling each other by registering disapproval of 'silly' behaviour. This frees the co-leaders to offer help with individual activities and stimulate discussion. On the whole this censuring has been accepted well by group members as it was usually undertaken by the more self-assured members whose standing in the group was high. In one group some members challenged us to say how we planned the sessions and allocated tasks.

Dependency/Task orientation

The highly structured leadership style adopted here tends to generate a certain amount of initial dependency, whilst task orientation is affected by the level of intelligence and stage of emotional development of some individual members.

As previously mentioned, with rare exceptions group members are initially very compliant. Discussion is sometimes limited by lack of both confidence and mutual trust but this improves noticeably in later sessions. Dependency upon the group leaders begins to lessen somewhat by the third session as the members begin to emerge as a 'group'. Orientation to the task is still less consistent by this session partly, we suspect, because of the conflict and jockeying for position between group members and partly because we are dealing with some slightly uncomfortable areas. Perhaps we have not yet got the content of this session right.

In subsequent sessions all group members seem to take more readily to set tasks. Perhaps by this stage they feel more settled or the tasks are more interesting. As the sessions progress, all members seem more confident to participate in the discussions and take part in the activities.

In one group, the sixth session proved something of a turning point for one of the teenage boys who, in previous sessions, wore his hair quite long; because he tended to look down most of the time his eyes were virtually obscured by his fringe. In Session Six he arrived with his hair cut and confident enough to hold his head up and look at other members and the leaders when speaking. Of itself, this change may seem trivial, but it was dramatic progress for him. There was no evidence to attribute this change solely to his attendance at the group but it seemed likely that it contributed. (A number of residential social work staff have reported to us a noticeable rise in self-esteem on the part of the majority of teenagers who attended.) By the last session, whilst members still seem dependent on the leaders in terms of the latter prescribing the activities of the group, in social and emotional terms they appear much less so.

SUMMARY

Though foster care theory forms the background for the kind of preparatory work described here, a knowledge of groupwork theory and of groupwork models is also necessary. In the first place such knowledge makes it possible to choose the model most suited to the needs of the participants and to fulfilling the aims of the group. It also helps one to be prepared for the stages that groups go through and to know roughly what to expect. With this knowledge it is also possible to think through problems before they occur in order to avoid them, or have alternative strategies ready or even decide to ride out the storm. The well-being of members can depend on this knowledge. The absence of ready-made practice models for this kind of work has meant a fair amount of initial experimentation but we also benefited from the experience of similar groups already run by some other departments around the country. Our model falls into what Brown (1979) describes as 'problem solving, task centred and social skills models'.

In planning the groups we went for a very structured, closed and task-centred group to produce a safe atmosphere that would contain the fears and anxieties of members. We also concentrated on providing a variety of activities in order to hold attention and cater for the needs of all members. Our experience bears out the necessity of continuing to do so. It is also important not to underestimate the propensity of members to learn from each other and to actively encourage the sharing of their ideas and experience.

Unlike some other models where the co-leaders separate out the roles of 'nurturer' and 'task-master' we chose not to do so. Instead, in every session we each assume responsibility for certain tasks and at other times take on the role of nurturer. This seems to work well and avoids any type casting. It has also become obvious for us from the level of help some group members require, that two group leaders are very necessary. Besides helping to promote better group interaction, it is also mutually supportive and responsibility is shared. We have also found it valuable to meet after each group meeting and for a group 'consultant' to join us to provide a more objective and detached perception. Through experience we learned the importance of being flexible enough to adapt our programme to the needs of each individual group and to select activities with which both leaders feel comfortable.

A possible criticism that could be levelled at us is that there are too few group sessions, especially when account is taken of the time the group takes to reach a 'performing' stage. We have given this aspect some serious thought and, for a variety of reasons, have decided not to increase the number of sessions at present. Feedback from the group members indicates that young people do find the group a useful and enjoyable experience. This is also borne out by the low drop-out rate (only two members out of six groups) and high attendance levels. Initial reactions to the meetings are often very guarded and we stand or fall by our ability to engage the group. As one teenager put it: 'I only intended to go to the Preparation Group for the first session to see how I would like it and also because my social worker and primary worker from the family group home thought it was a good idea. I found that the first session was interesting and as the sessions progressed I decided to follow it through.'

Another shared this feeling: 'I thought it was going to be dead boring but it came out very interesting – fun in fact.'

We have come to expect that a significant proportion of the group members will decide against fostering, for a variety of reasons. One young person commented: 'The Group made me realize I love my parents and no matter what they did to me or I did to them, they were still my parents and I cared about them.' Others acknowledged that the group was instrumental in helping them to reach decisions: 'I would advise teenagers to come to the group as it helps you to understand what you want – you have time to think instead of rushing into things.' For those who are able to look back on the group and see how well things have worked out for them there is a sense of satisfaction: 'In my place what I wished for is happening and it is pleasing to know that you have achieved what you wanted.'

Although we would not always claim that things work out quite as well as this, feedback from social workers and our own experience convinces us that the group makes an important contribution to the preparation of teenagers considering family placement. We would also agree with Lindsey-Smith (1980) who wrote that 'the revelations of the children's group have shown us that it is futile to concentrate on families while we leave the children unprepared'.

9

Groupwork with black children in white foster homes
Audrey Mullender

INTRODUCTION

Against a background of the disproportionate number of black children and young people in care[1], and of the growing confirmation in the literature that black families can be found to foster or adopt many of them once special efforts are made[2] (such as recognizing the particular strengths of black families[3]) this chapter will focus on the far more neglected area of meeting the needs of those black children who have already become established in long-term white foster homes. (A later chapter will consider the needs of their white foster parents.) Many such children will remain in their white homes for the foreseeable future, even where further transracial placements are most actively opposed (Small, 1985, p. 11; Small, 1986a, p. 11). There is, therefore, an urgent need to develop practice which can help to foster their awareness of their cultural and racial origins, and of themselves as young black people growing up in a predominantly white, racist society.

A good deal of individual work with young, black people has already begun to tackle the difficulties which can result from transracial placement (Fratter, 1986; Mennell, 1986; Maximé, 1986; Maximé, 1987). These difficulties arise in three particular areas:

(a) identity and self-image: black children, not uncommonly, try to scrub, bleach or powder themselves white to be like their foster families (Ahmed, 1981, pp. 139-40; Adeniji, 1983, p. 12) and feel uncomfortable in later life when they cannot easily find acceptance amongst black people (see Parr in Black and In Care Steering Group, 1985, p. 38; Association of Black Social Workers and Allied Professions (ABSWAP), 1983, pp. 7-8; see also Divine, 1983a and 1983b commenting on Gill and Jackson, 1983);

127

(b) the inability of many white parents to teach black children how to survive the impact of racialist abuse and prejudice (Cheetham, 1981, p. 57, quoting the National Association of Black Social Workers in the USA; James, 1981, pp. 15-16; Children's Legal Centre, 1985, p. 7);

(c) the ignorance of many white families about black families and their unease about inviting them on access visits (Loftus, 1986, pp. 26-7).

The chief innovation of this chapter is to consider how groupwork, rather than an individual approach, has been successfully used to tackle these current criticisms of transracial placements, and to meet black children's needs more adequately in the context of their long-term white placements.

The Ebony Young People's Group

Accounts of the first Ebony group for black children fostered by white families, which ran for six weeks in 1983, have been published in two journal articles (Mullender and Miller, 1985; Miller, 1985), but the second Ebony Young People's Group, which ran in late 1985, has not previously been described in published material other than a departmental report (Nottinghamshire Social Services Department 1986). The aims established in advance of the second group, by the group-workers, were mainly to create a forum for self-awareness/black awareness; to develop an acceptance of, and a pride in being black, and to begin to develop survival skills against racism. In total, the group's purpose was to instil pride, and to help the children to become strong black individuals.

The young people's group consisted of youngsters referred by their social workers. At the planning stage, there were thought to be approximately 87 transracial placements amongst the children placed with foster parents by the local authority. All the children referred to the group were of Afro-Caribbean or mixed Afro-Caribbean/white parentage, as were the leaders. Owing to the very specific material to be covered, it was not intended that Asian children should be included in the group and they are, in any case, under-represented in the care of the authority concerned. From the initial 17 referrals (11 female and 6 male), it was originally intended to form two young people's groups, but because of the drop in numbers at the first meeting it was decided to combine all those present into just one young people's group. The main reason for the drop was given as prior commitments. It is not known whether negative feelings on the part of the foster parents prevented any young people from attending. In the event, a maximum of 10 young people attended any one session, made up of eight female and two male members, with a wide age range of between ten and eighteen years.

All but two of the group members were in white foster placements, a fair distance outside the city centre in predominantly white areas, but they were the responsibility of three inner city social services areas whose staff had originally made the placements. The young people had been in their white foster homes in the region of nine to fifteen years, so it can be seen that these were well-established placements. The remaining two teenagers had been in similar foster homes until a year or two previously. One had moved, when a placement disrupted after 14 years, to a community home in the inner city. The other had been in a black foster home for two years after living in a children's home and a series of white foster homes.

When the two groups were merged the leadership team also combined forces and included three fieldworkers (two female, one male) and three residential workers (two male, one female). Although a ratio of 6 workers to 10 young people is high, it emerged later as having been justified, firstly because it gave the flexibility to split into sub-groups for certain tasks, and secondly because it offered a greater range of worker skills. Each team included both male and female, and both field and residential workers. The young people themselves enjoyed having six leaders since it gave them a choice of black adults to whom they could relate. They also warmly appreciated the relative youth of the workers because, as the youngsters put it, they were not 'fuddy duddies'. Indeed the leaders were able to join in boisterous games and also, in a more serious vein, to understand the experience of being young and black in contemporary Britain.

The young people's group was more enjoyable, both to run and to belong to, than the foster parents' group, and even when a number of foster parents dropped out of their group, their respective foster children did not cease to attend theirs. The young people's shared experiences emerged right from the start, which made it easier for them to gel as a group than it was for their foster parents. Even those children who were more resistant to examining their own attitudes about blackness could just join in and enjoy group games and experiential exercises, so they were able to find their own level in the group without group without preventing the others from learning.

There were eight weekly group sessions followed by a joint day out for the young people's and foster parents' groups together with all the leaders. Each group meeting was preceded by a workers' planning meeting and followed by an evaluation session for the workers and their respective consultants. These took place separately for the workers with the young people and the workers with the foster parents. There was also a considerable amount of research undertaken, prior to the sessions, into each particular topic to be covered. These topics were influenced significantly by the earlier Ebony group (Mullender and Miller, 1985) but with some changes and additions, reflecting in part the increase from six group meetings to eight. The detailed account of the group sessions which follows, is based closely on the worker team's own report (Notts. S.S.D., 1986, pp. 7-15).

Week One – 'Introduction to the group'

The group leaders introduced themselves and explained the layout of the building. The group then played a name game to learn each other's names. A discussion ensued on why there was a need for such a group, the sorts of topics to be covered in the following weeks, and the fact that members themselves could also raise matters of interest to them. After a break for coffee, the two groups of young people and their foster parents together watched a video on racial prejudice, but returned to their separate groups to look at the issues raised by the video, such as the frequent negative racial stereotyping in the media. A 'brainstorm' technique was used to allow all the young people to pool definitions they had come across of the words 'black' and 'white' in everyday language, and also to list jobs they could think of which black and white people are employed to do. Finally, there was consideration of how the young people wished to be described.

The underlying aims of this first session were to begin to establish a shared group identity and to determine the level of black awareness amongst group members. This emerged as rather low, although some of the older ones pretended to be very 'aware' and 'streetwise'. The experiences they claimed to have had were all expressed through clichés – about hanging around in certain parts of the inner city, going to blues parties, and the like – but, when pressed, it emerged not only that they only knew white people, but that they appeared to be afraid of black people. The older group members were not alone in making unrealistic claims. A number of the younger children, too, when asked how many black friends they had, answered 'loads' and when asked exactly how many said 'Oh, lots and lots', and then were unable to name any, not surprisingly since they lived in practically all-white areas and were virtually the only black children in their respective schools.

The younger children were extremely 'unaware' of cultural and racial issues, but soon became thirsty for knowledge, chorusing 'Tell us more', 'What is it like (to be this, to do that)', etc. Initially, all the young people were rather quiet and the group was slow to get started. During the brainstorm on definitions, on the whole the young people gave negative images of black people and none of them wished to be called black, many preferring terms such as 'coloured', 'mixed race' or 'half-caste'[4]. As regards jobs that black and white people do, no one mentioned social work as a job that black people do, despite having six black social workers as group leaders! From the discussion after the video on prejudice, it emerged that all the group members had had to deal with racism, hostility and prejudice themselves.

Week Two – 'Fostering'

The workers' planning meeting had felt strongly that this second session should start by picking up further on the negative assumptions which had been demonstrated by the children in the first week, and also the common experiences they had highlighted. The group was bigger on the second occasion, reaching its maximum size of ten. From then on, all the young people attended, with the single exception of one who gave advance notice of missing one week. This is probably a good measure of the success of the group and of the commitment of the young people to it. A further test of the group in engaging the young people was that communication was initiated more readily this time, no doubt also because some of the members now knew each other. The leaders felt it was appropriate to revert to their original intention of splitting the group into two, and this was done on the original basis of age (with the dividing line at 14), since 10-year-olds and 17-year-olds have so little in common. Building on the shared experience of racism revealed in the first session, each sub-group was asked to suggest ways of dealing with racist comments and racist behaviour, other than retaliating in anger. Here, as throughout the life of the young people's group, the personal experiences of the black leaders were crucial, and one is reminded of the debate referred to earlier as to whether black parents teach their children survival skills which white substitute parents do not automatically have.

After the coffee break, the young people stayed in two smaller groups and moved on to the material which had originally been intended for this second session, which was to consider both the positive and negative aspects of a black home and of a white home. These were then shared when the total group reconvened. The aim here was to look at individual experiences of transracial and, in one case, same race placements. This produced mixed feelings from the young people who were, however, able to be honest about their views. One member stated: 'If you were in a black home no one would know you were a foster child because you and your foster parents would be the same colour.' This child, it emerged, had been laughed at by friends when seen out shopping with a white foster mother. On the whole, however, the youngsters showed fierce allegiance to their white foster parents. Finally, there was an evaluation exercise in which members were asked to list their likes and dislikes of the session.

Week Three – 'History of the Caribbean'

This topic was also covered by the earlier Ebony group in 1983, and is seen as offering fundamentally important information for young people of Afro-Caribbean origin which – as was clear from the fact that most of the group members did not know which island they originated from – frequently was not provided in a transracial home setting. The group session for the young people on this occasion included a geographical synopsis of the West Indian islands. To begin with, the children were asked to name as many islands as they could. The group examined on a map where the West Indies are situated and discussed how black people arrived there. A contemporary black perspective was also applied to the races, culture, industry, and other features of the modern-day Caribbean. After the break, the children were again sub-divided to complete a questionnaire designed to show how much they could remember about the material covered earlier. Discussion was more productive in the smaller groups since each child could be more fully involved.

The aim of this session had been to stress 'positive' images of the West Indies and also to present a black emphasis on their history. Like all educators, the groupworkers struggled to find ways of presenting their material so as to make it lively and interesting. The questionnaire contributed towards this aim, since it was used as a game, whilst at the same time making it apparent that much of the information had been retained and assimilated. Many of the children had never learnt from which island their families originated, which was unfortunate since it would have helped to make the islands more real to them. This session sent a number of the young people away with the enthusiasm to seek further information about their roots.

Week Four – 'Music'

Once again, the idea for this session was carried over from the earlier Ebony group two years previously. Its impact on both occasions was resounding in all senses of the word. Each group leader talked about, then played tapes of different aspects of black music and dance, encompassing jazz, gospel music, funk, soul, reggae, calypso, body popping, hip hop, breakdancing and dub poetry. Musical instruments had been hired from a local black arts' centre and the real success of the session lay in the fact that the young people could experiment with these and begin to make their own music. Unsure and reserved at first, for example when asked to read dub poetry aloud West Indian style, the young people gradually lost their embarrassment and eventually an improvised 'jam' session was in full swing. The informality, fun and element of risk-taking in these activities helped to create bonds between the group members as well as between members and leaders. On the more serious side, the importance of black music within the development of music in general was addressed, as was the major contribution which black performers have made to music, and black artists to wider culture.

Week Five – 'Hair and skin care'

The format for this meeting with the young people was based on a visit by a professional black hairdresser who brought products along for the young people to experiment with. She described types of black hair, showing suitable ways of caring for and styling it, and also demonstrated basic skin care and black make-up on one of the female group members. Again, group participation in this essentially practical session was at a high level, with a lively exchange of questions and answers, though the wide age range of the children meant that the make-up and hair styles were not suitable for some. For most of the young people, the session built on and reinforced quite a good standard of hair and skin care, although many of the children washed their hair more often than was good for it, since frequent washing loses all the natural oils. When black children do exhibit tangled hair, as can happen in transracial placements, it is an indication that additional information on hair care and styling is needed.

Week Six – 'Life snake and role-play'

Because the 'Black and In Care' video could not be shown, instead the young people split into their two sub-groups. The older group drew life snakes, that is, representations of their lives to date, plotting negative and positive experiences along the body of a snake. Not all the children felt able to participate. From individual discussions, it emerged that they did not want the others to see the more painful or distressing elements of their lives, or the number of moves they had experienced. Also in this older sub-group was a sibling group, who decided to draw their snake together as a joint effort, and then used it as a vehicle to piece their life together to date. They had been placed in different foster homes and had never before had the opportunity to talk together in this way.

Meanwhile, the younger children attempted a role-play in which they took on the roles of their own foster parents. This gave the workers a good deal of information about the children's home lives. For example, it was clear that in one family the foster child was treated differently from the other children and, in another, the child was not encouraged to have black visitors beyond the immediate family. One child was particularly helped by her role-play which brought out her difficult behaviour at home. The workers talked to her – still in the role of her foster father – who told them she was 'a real pain'. They then asked 'him' how 'he' handled his foster daughter, and 'he' replied: 'Oh well, I love (that is "cuddle") her and all that, I don't beat her.' So they asked 'Oh, don't you? Why is that?' and were surprised at the insight of this relatively young child who answered: 'She's not the kind who responds to that', and was helped to reflect on the impact of her behaviour on her foster family and its meaning for herself.

Some children had fears that if they took part in the role-play and showed their real feelings, these would be reported back to their foster parents. They did not all respond to reassurance that the group was confidential, thus illustrating the worrying extent to which so many of the children in the group carried responsibility for their foster parents' feelings.

Week Seven – 'Africa and slavery'

The intention of this session was again to stress positive images of black people, this time in the context of Africa and African life, and also to convey a black historical perspective on the effects of slavery and on black participation in the movement to repeal the laws which allowed it. The guest speaker was a teacher on African history. He opened with a geographical synopsis of Africa and then showed a video which gave a historical appraisal. The wide age range of the audience made his task extremely difficult and, unfortunately, some of the information was pitched too high for some of the youngest members, although the older ones said they had learned a great deal. Nevertheless, all joined in the question and answer period, and ensuing discussion. Since so much factual information had been presented, the group leaders prepared a simple summary which was distributed the following week.

Week Eight – 'Evaluation'

The final session again divided the young people into two groups to consider their likes and dislikes arising from each of the preceding weeks. Reasons for preferences were also sought, as were alternative suggestions. The workers found this evaluation by members to be very helpful, and it also impressed on group members the vast amount of material they had covered over the eight weeks of the group. The complete young people's group then reassembled and heard outline plans for the forthcoming day trip. Finally, they played their favourite games from preceding weeks.

The group meetings were followed by an outing of the young people, foster parents and leaders from both groups. Everyone enjoyed a visit to the Commonwealth Institute in London, where there are exhibits and displays on the population, life-style and other features of every Commonwealth country. Afterwards the whole party dined at a Caribbean restaurant.

Some general conclusions

Overall, the young people's group meetings attempted to cover a wide range of factual material and also to deal with the feelings it aroused. The use of speakers, audio-visual aids and packages of material to take home, all helped to vary the presentation of direct information. The group also created the opportunity for more informal interaction in recognition of the young people's ages and, in some cases, limited concentration spans. Each week there was a coffee break part way through the two-hour meeting, and usually some games to conclude.

One of the major initial difficulties for the young people attending the Ebony group was in relation to black adults. This was, no doubt, one of the causes of the fairly frequent silences in the first few weeks. Other reasons may have included the fact that the young people were in care, regardless of their colour. Stein (1983, p. 97) concludes from his groupwork with young people in care, which the present author has also experienced, that: 'many new members of in-care groups lack confidence and self-esteem. They find it very difficult to contribute, to talk about issues and exchange views. This is partly a predictable response to the newness of the group situation, but it is also a reflection of their experiences of care'. Stein goes on to suggest some of the reasons why being in care undermines young people's confidence, for example, through the stress and upheaval which care implies. The interaction through games and exercises was found to be a valuable means of breaking the ice for the young people, both between themselves and the group leaders and with each other, since, in their predominantly white environments, few of them had any black friends. The uneven gender balance in the young people's group worsened from the initially expected 11 female and 6 male, to the actual 8 female and only 2 male, which left the two boys noticeably isolated. Since boys appear to be more difficult to place in foster homes than girls, and since more of them failed to attend the group (though a number had good reasons), this uneven ratio might be a factor to guard against in other, similar groups.

The group workers felt that the eight-week length of the group, and also the two hours of each weekly session, were both too short, given the amount of material which was covered, and the need to give adequate time and space to the feelings it aroused and to the young people's questioning and absorption of new ideas. The group leaders exercised their skills in carrying over and developing issues from one week to the next and, where necessary, amended their planned content accordingly. Some major questions arise from this conclusion that the group was too short including, firstly, the group's place in relation to the individual work being undertaken with each young person in his or her foster family and, secondly, the group's central purpose and function. Groupwork with black children in white foster homes cannot replace individual work with the young person. Rather, that is always the necessary starting point for assessing and beginning to meet a child's needs, and it will normally also continue in parallel with the child's membership of a group like Ebony. The success of a young person's participation in this type of group could also be greatly enhanced by preparation undertaken by the child's own social worker. Not only could the child be helped to make best use of the group, but maximum information given to the group leaders about the child would assist them in involving the child as fully as possible. Information also needs to be two-way. A child's experience of belonging to the group would inevitably arouse feelings, ideas and confusions which he or she and the individual social worker could work on together, perhaps more fruitfully than any of their earlier work, provided that the social worker was kept fully abreast of what the group was covering. Information of this sort should only be communicated with the child's knowledge and consent, however, since otherwise assurances of confidentiality (offered, for example, to those who feared revelation to their foster parents if they participated in a role-play) would not be in good faith. Finally, the individual social worker needs to offer follow-up work in relation to a young person's needs as identified in the group, in terms of his or her stage of cultural knowledge and racial identity.

SUMMARY

Following the undoubted success of both Ebony groups for young black people (and of the group for white foster parents), there is a strong feeling, amongst those who have been most closely involved with it, that Ebony should become a 'mainstream' project. In other words, a cross-area structure should be ironed out and Ebony should have guaranteed support to run, probably on an annual basis, with black workers released from other duties for this purpose. The fact that Ebony has so far developed in an *ad hoc* manner, seen by some as tokenism, may reflect not only its relative newness but also a general feature of groupwork. As Brown (1979, p. 2) has remarked: 'Groupwork is often viewed as a slightly esoteric "optional extra", something of a luxury to be indulged in a social worker's spare time, and a relatively low priority for resources.' Set against the level of need which has been shown to exist, however, groupwork should be recognised as a powerful means of offering more practical, cultural, and racial information and skills, and asisting young black people to develop a strong black identity.

Because these concerns are so important, they should be the proper goals of social work intervention rather than sticks with which to beat white foster parents who have thought it best to ignore them. There is now a feeling in some quarters in relation to Ebony, that there should be a comprehensive expectation that all black children in white placements, and their white foster parents, should attend Ebony-type groups, unless there is a definite reason why this would not be possible or advisable. In addition to black groupworkers, managers, and consultants for these groups, there needs to be training for all social workers who would be in a position to make referrals, and who would therefore also be responsible for preparatory and follow-up work with individual young people and their foster parents. A 'Black and In Care' style of group should almost certainly be separate from this provision since it would work towards different goals, and would perhaps be best located in the voluntary sector. Also, it would serve black teenagers in a range of placements, not just transracial ones, so would not be the kind of specialist provision that Ebony has been designed to be.

Whatever the shape of future groupwork with black children in care in Nottinghamshire, and there is still a huge unmet need, other local authorities and voluntary agencies with responsibility for black children in white placements, should also begin to examine the provision they are making and to implement comprehensively structured policies to fill the identified gaps. Groups like Ebony can, of course, only be one factor in the building of positive self-image and cultural identity for black teenagers in Britain. The educational curriculum – including the 'hidden curriculum' of attitudes and behaviour – in school, and the policies of other public bodies such as the police and the courts, all have a more wide-reaching and major impact. Nevertheless, for a particular group of young people, those who are transracially placed, and who are the responsibility of social work agencies, Ebony does offer an exciting model for future developments.

ACKNOWLEDGEMENT

This chapter and the chapter on foster parents are, in a very real sense, the joint product of the innovatory ideas and practice achievements of all those concerned with the Nottinghamshire Social Services Department Ebony Project and of my own attempts to record their work for others to read and, we hope, to emulate. I should like to express my thanks and indebtedness to all the following:

Leaders of the young people's group: Tony Atkin, Chris Mundell, Jasmine Nembhard, Annette Smith, Dave Weaver and Elaine White.

Leaders of the foster parents' group: Sadie Henry, Ann Newman and Dianne Skerritt.

Managers of the project: Jo Browne, Sarah Davis and Margaret McGlade.

Consultant to the young people's group: Clem Benjamin.

Notes

1. See, for example, Knight, 1977, p. 18; Lindsay Smith, 1979, p. 6; Association of Black Social Workers and Allied Professions (ABSWAP), 1983, pp. 6-7; Stone, 1983, p. 4; House of Commons Social Services Committee, 1984, p. cxix; Cheetham, 1986, pp. 28-9.

2. See, for example, Gayes, 1975; Ahmed, 1978 and 1980; James, 1979 and 1981; Arnold, 1982; Association of British Adoption and Fostering Agencies, 1981; Cheetham, 1981, pp. 49-50 and 63-73; Fitzgerald, 1981; Small, 1982 and 1986b, p. 83; ABSWAP, 1983, p. 6; Brunton and Welch, 1983; Lambeth Black Children's Project, 1983; Murray, 1983, pp. 15-16; Schroeder and Lightfoot, 1983; Schroeder, Lightfoot and Rees, 1985; Cann, 1984, pp. 44-5; Bradford Fostering and Adoption Unit, 1985; Divine, 1985, p. 9; Skerritt and Watkins, 1986.

3. See, for example, Brunton and Welch, 1983, p. 18; Schroeder, Lightfoot and Rees, 1985, pp. 50-2; Divine, 1985, pp. 7-8; Randmawa, 1985, pp. 42-3.

4. The preferred terms are now 'black' and 'mixed parentage'. ABSWAP (1983, p. 10) explains that:

    The concept 'mixed parentage' should be used instead of 'mixed race', since the former does not imply the race superior quotient

139

implied by the latter . . . We should be constantly aware that when . . . some social workers use the term 'mixed race' they do not mean the child of Indian and African parents nor Chinese and a person of African descent. They generally mean a 'white' person and any other person who is not white.

The term 'mixed parentage', on the other hand, would apply equally well in any of the circumstances listed. The term 'black' should always be used unless there is a particular need to distinguish an individual or group as 'mixed parentage', 'Asian', 'Afro-Caribbean', etc.

Section 3

Post-placement and post-adoption support groups

10

Introduction

John Triseliotis

The development of post-placement and post-adoption support groups was bound to follow the introduction of preparatory ones. It was an acknowledgement that preparation by itself was not enough and that for the gains to be sustained it was necessary to make available a range of post-placement services in the form of support and consultation. Furthermore, that some of these services could be provided more effectively in groups, thus supplementing individual efforts. As with preparatory groups, the underlying premise was that those fostering or adopting, particularly where the children have special needs, should not be expected to shoulder alone the responsibilities of caring and of parenthood without a range of external supports being made available. It was also argued that special needs children can present problems of management of behaviour or handicap which can be demanding of their new families' coping strengths. Crowley (1982) supports the idea of post-placement support, based on her findings that the influence of pre-placement training courses such as 'Parenting Plus' fades with time and appears remote. Jones (1975) concluded from his study that the lack of post-placement support was a vital factor in the decision of foster parents to cease fostering.

Macaskill's study (1984) highlighted the fact that adoptive and foster parents catering for special needs children see themselves as having to cope with a difficult task for which 'they require a range of practical supportive services, counselling on how to handle certain behaviours displayed by the children and also understanding and appreciation of

143

what they do'. Cautley (1980), interpreting findings from her foster care study, also comes out in strong support of post-placement services. Yates (1985), in a recent follow-up study of adoptive and foster placements made by Lothian Region, remarked on the basis of comments made by carers that 'social work intervention appeared crucial in maintaining the placement, especially when difficult behaviour was occurring . . . without this support some of the families might have given up'. What is even more interesting is Yates's finding that children placed for adoption or fostering did not differ in characteristics and behaviour.

Post-adoption services

The provision of post-adoption services to parents and children was being encouraged even in the days when adoption was about healthy infants and few, if any, complications were expected. Most agencies, though, did not go beyond asking adopters to keep in touch and not hesitate to approach them if they needed any help. A study by Gohros (1967) revealed that the attitude of adopters to post-adoption help was usually coloured by their experience during the post-placement period. In effect, those who found the contact useful during this stage were more likely to go for help after the adoption was completed, and the reverse was equally true.

Picton (1977), in a well-documented article, argues that the past practice of asking adopters to seek further help 'if there were problems' prevented many of them from seeking support or information. As far back as 1959, Brown stressed the need for post-adoption services on the ground that, regardless of the quality of selection and other services, it is impossible to predict the outcome of adoption and that nothing can make up for the reality of the child 'actually living with the new family and their adjustment to each other'. Kirk (1964) and Gohros (1967) put forward the idea that role handicap, the way adoption was practised at the time, the strivings of adopters to be accepted as parents and the wish to preserve some autonomy over their lives and parenting, militate against further contact with adoption agencies. An example of this is provided by Macaskill (1984) who found that, of those who adopted mentally handicapped children and joined local support groups consisting mainly of natural parents, some, though not all, left the group. They felt uncomfortable because of what they saw as the 'strange looks from natural parents, some of whom found it incredible that anyone could choose to adopt a handicapped child'.

If there were strong arguments for providing post-adoption services in the case of baby adoption, these appear even more compelling in the case of present day adoption. In spite of the pre-placement preparation provided by many agencies, nothing can quite prepare for the actual experience of parenting older children with a history of experiences, not infrequently negative ones. Kagan and Reid (1986) claim that their American study supports the need for a continuation of services to be provided to biological parents, to adoptive parents and to youths both before and after adoptive placement. Finkelstein (1982) and Donley (1983) call for 'post-legalisation counselling and even reinstitutionalisation' to be available to adoptive parents in an effort to maintain a youth's ties with an adoptive family. Sandler (1979) claims that the connection of the adoptive family to social support networks has direct and indirect influence on the functioning of children and parents, and Veroff et al. (1981) comment that the growth of the self-help movement highlights the importance of informal services to families. Macaskill (1984) also concludes from her study of 37 mentally handicapped children adopted through the London-based agency Parents for Children, that in view of the complex and serious difficulties facing many of the families after the first two years of placement, a long-term support service is essential. After outlining a number of important concrete services she refers to the beneficial value of local support groups consisting mainly of adoptive parents.

Post-placement groups for foster parents

In foster care, unlike adoption, agency-continued responsibility and involvement is a statutory obligation. Furthermore, there is increasing evidence that post-placement support appears to be most crucial during the early months of the placement. Stone and Stone (1983) found, for example, that social-worker support, rapport building and input were highly predictive of placement stability. Similar evidence comes from Cautley (1980). Though social workers always tried to provide some form of individual post-placement support, the idea of groups is more recent.

The original idea for setting up foster carers' support groups originated in the USA but they did not become widespread here until the 1980s. The current practice is for groups to have a continued life, with the expectation that at least 'contract' type foster carers will attend regularly. An early American example of a post-placement support group is described by Bailey (1969). This was a programme of six sessions set up for existing foster mothers. The purpose of the group was unclear but the participating foster mothers wanted to talk about the children's problems and about the natural parents, and above all they were seeking reassurance that they were doing a good job. Hazel (1981), who recruited professional foster carers for the Kent scheme, saw such groups as 'people helping each other' with the focus of the meetings on 'describing and evaluating the work being done'. Through such meetings families would share skills, come to feel less isolated and develop a corporate identity, becoming a kind of 'artificial tribe'. She still saw a role for social workers as 'convenors and enablers'. Though agencies expect attendance and encourage participation they are far from viewing it as compulsory. Furthermore, attendance at post-placement support groups seems to be largely related to role perception and function.

Some issues concerning purpose, content and organization

Though somewhat different considerations are involved in the setting up of post-adoption support groups compared to post-placement ones for foster carers, nevertheless both types of groups share many characteristics. For example, the ultimate purpose of both is to sustain and enhance the placement for the well-being of those involved. Another common objective is the provision of support to both groups of 'substitute' parents. The concept of 'support' has no agreed definition, as Jana Brown also points out in this Section, but in this context 'to feel supported' implies: being listened to and appreciated for efforts made or for trying to cope with a situation; feeling understood when sharing an issue or a problem; being encouraged in one's efforts and being valued by one's peers. The provision of practical resources or the linking of group members to such resources is part of the same continuum of support. The term 'support' is used collectively by agencies to describe opportunities provided at the post-adoption and post-placement levels, but experience suggests that 'contract' foster carers, in particular, expect something more than just support. They are there mainly to find out how to handle children.

Post-placement support groups offer opportunities to those under-taking similar tasks to share and learn from each other, and a forum within which complex feelings can be shared and dealt with. Compared to preparatory groups, post-placement ones move decidedly into the area of problem-formulation and problem-solving, with actual rather than hypothetical situations. In brief, they offer a forum for support, group consultation and counselling, information-giving and the provision of training. Concerns, difficulties and even achievements can be shared and, where appropriate, solutions sought. This approach acknowledges that there are both strengths and weaknesses in a situation and that participants can help each other to recognize them, thus broadening their choices and their coping repertoire. The groups provide appreciation from peers and, more important, understanding and support when the going is tough or when a placement breaks down and there are feelings of guilt and badness all round. The knowledge and skills of social workers are seen as supplementary to those of the carers. Others, from within and outside the agency, can also contribute towards general educational and training objectives, including talks and video or tape presentations. Unlike preparatory groups which are time-limited, post-placement ones for foster carers are currently more likely to be open-ended. This presents the organizers with the additional task of finding ways to sustain the interest of members over lengthy periods of time.

Post-adoption and post-placement support groups share many features of purpose and content but also have a number of differences arising from the different nature of the task. For a start the two groups of carers approach membership of support groups with not exactly similar expectations. Adoptive parents, for example, are under no 'obligation' to attend such groups. Their attendance arises chiefly from their own perception of their needs. Neither do they have professional expectations in terms of training and development like, for example, 'contract' foster parents. For them a support group is meant to be there to be used if and when needed rather than as a matter of course. They look upon the group as offering them opportunities for peer support over childcare concerns and as keeping them in touch with social workers and other 'experts' who can again be consulted if and when needed. Unlike foster carers' groups, their attendance is likely to be more episodic but perhaps not inappropriately so.

As a result of the differences outlined there is more scope for a post-adoption group developing eventually into a 'self-help' group than for a foster carers' one doing so. Though adoptive parents may need agency assistance to set up their support group, as in the case of the Lothian Adopters' Group described in this Section by Sandra Hutton, nevertheless adopters see themselves as running their own show. Additional help from social workers and other professionals is not shunned but viewed as essential for success. Douglas (1986), commenting on 'self-help' groups which are peer-led, remarked that they have never been well investigated or studied, so we know very little of how such leaders are chosen. In his view there is an apparent dislike of the idea of leadership and the use of power.

In contrast to post-adoption groups, the nature of the fostering task militates against the idea of a 'self-help' group as understood in the literature. Neither is there a rush among foster parents either to lead groups or take full responsibility for running them. Foster care, whether at the individual or group level, implies a shared responsibility between social workers and carers. Though nothing could stop any group of people or carers from forming their own 'self-help' group, its value in this context would be limited. A more appropriate model is one of partnership which includes the joint planning, organizing and running of support groups. The leadership and co-leadership of the group can then be drawn from the ranks of both social workers and foster carers. Such an arrangement gives practical expression to the notion of a 'colleague'-type relationship between the two groups. More experienced carers could be allocated more formal roles and responsibilities, that could involve them in the planning and running of preparatory and post-placement groups and in acting as consultants to new foster parents on an individual or small group basis.

The contributors

Dick O'Brien describes the running and life of a post-placement support group and reflects on some of the organizational and practice issues. Jana Brown provides a similar example but focuses particularly on the planning and organizational aspects of setting up and running such a group in a rural area. Sandra Hutton writes from the perspective of being an adoptive parent and a part-time employee of Lothian Region who has been instrumental in setting up the Lothian Adopters' Group. Finally, Audery Mullender describes the use of groupwork with transracial foster parents, as a potentially effective way of reaching beyond the improvement of their practical knowledge about black cultures to their feelings and attitudes.

11

Post-placement support groups for community carers

Dick O'Brien

INTRODUCTION

Many professional foster-parent schemes have post-placement support groups and the purpose of this chapter is to examine the rationale, content, processes and techniques of these groups. Since this is the term I use in my own work I shall refer to professional foster-parents as 'community carers'. They are paid a fee to care for children who usually display behaviour or emotional problems. Different schemes will operate differently, but a support group of community carers is one which meets regularly to discuss issues relating to the young people placed with them, so that the carers will find mutual support, learn from each other and the staff and develop their problem-solving potential. Such groups seem to fit best within the framework of an educational, consultative group and bear a particular resemblance to group supervision/consultation in social work: here participants bring issues to do with their work to the group for discussion and a designated social worker acts as the formal leader of the group. Post-placement support groups are not the same as group counselling or psychotherapy groups, since the orientation is that those attending are akin to colleagues who require skilled assistance to carry out a demanding task, rather than being clients requiring help with personal difficulties. Within this framework of a 'colleague' relationship, there is always an important element of personal support and development, but these are by-products which result from the process of assisting the carers to carry out their tasks. Inevitably some of the processes generated in these groups, their dynamics, difficulties and potential benefits, bear some similarity to those observed in group counselling, such as the influence for personal change of a peer group.

149

Purpose and underlying premise

Our post-placement group was set up in response to the need of carers for support and continued training. It is meant to generate peer support, problem-solving and learning. The underlying premise is that the carers, by undertaking the demanding task of caring and providing 'treatment' to children displaying a range of difficulties, require support, consultation and continual training. Though some of this can be provided on an individual basis, the group has been found to be a more effective and acceptable vehicle for the provision of these services. The group as a forum seems to make it easier for carers to share issues and difficulties and to provide or obtain support from peers undertaking a similar job. Such support appears particularly relevant when a carer faces a crisis with a young person or when a placement actually breaks down and the carers are left with a mixture of feelings. Such groups are also useful for introducing carers to new skills and knowledge that will improve their capacity to deal with the range of children's behaviour. Finally the group becomes a forum for communication between the carers and the agency on matters of mutual concern. In recognition of this a representative of the group sits on the Management Committee Scheme which considers the assessment and acceptance of new applicants.

Organization and structure

The group described here is task-centred and with no time limits. Though attendance is not compulsory there is an expectation that carers will attend, and most do. Members of the support group have previously attended preparatory groups which have helped to accustom them to work in groups. Where possible the life of the preparatory group is continued, now as a support group. Where the number of couples attending drops to six or eight, it may not be economical to continue and the members are then divided up amongst other support groups. This is not altogether bad as new membership can help break too much routine and stimulate a different type of discussion. On the whole, attendance by female carers is better than by males. This may have to do with traditional values of seeing women as more concerned with child rearing, as having more time with the young person and with shift work which makes attendance for some male carers difficult. Like Cautley (1980) we recognize the importance of involving men, but to make their attendance compulsory might elicit hostility and further dependences.

The actual structure of the group varies from scheme to scheme but in my own scheme we start groups on a shared-input model and meet fortnightly, though this can change over time and as the group wishes. As the carers develop more skills and greater confidence they may ask to meet less frequently. As organizer of the Community Carers' Scheme, I also act as convener and leader of the group. The groups meet from 7.30 to 9.30 pm with the formal work between 7.30 and 9.00 pm, followed by coffee. Each meeting starts by asking each member to say whether they require any of the group's time, and if so, a brief statement of what they wish to discuss. The remaining time is divided up between other different topics. If there are still important issues for discussion, the group can continue after 9.00 pm. If an issue cannot be dealt with in the time available or if it requires more individual work, then separate arrangements are made. Some topics may simply have to be held over for another meeting. Even where formal learning has been planned or a review of the group's processes, some time will still be reserved for possible urgent issues. If, through individual work, the group leader is aware of particular difficulties faced by a carer, it will still be left to the latter to raise these with the group or not.

Content

The group content is related to the purpose of the group, which is to provide a forum for problem-solving, support, information-giving and training.

Problem-solving refers to carers obtaining from each other, and sometimes others, ideas on how to handle particular situations, like glue sniffing or aggression. The carers are encouraged to air the problem, describe what has already been done or what they are contemplating doing about it. Group members may approve, be critical or offer suggestions. As most carers are parents themselves and some have brought up teenagers, there is no shortage of experience to be shared round. Unanimity does not always prevail, neither is there any responsibility placed on the presenter of a problem to follow a particular line. A couple may either go back to their original strategy or come to a new course of action as a result of the discussion. Often, however, carers are struck by a suggestion and become uplifted and encouraged by the thought that there is another approach to try out.

It is hard to separate problem-solving from support, as support is implied in all processes involving problem-solving. Perhaps in a group of this kind there is less direct problem-solving, with members being supported to find their own solutions. At one time a member may present an issue or a problem expecting support, whilst at another he is an enabler to somebody else. Each member can therefore be both a giver as well as a receiver, thus creating self-esteem and satisfaction which cannot easily be generated in relationships with individual social workers. Hearing other carers' problems can also help a couple place their difficulties in context. It has also been observed that group members store up learning from previous sessions and transfer it to subsequent problems which bear similarities.

Peer group support also takes place, partly through the act of talking to concerned others. There is a vital cathartic value for carers in being able to share difficult or worrying events with peers who may have gone through similar experiences. Such support may be independent of whether the group can assist with solving the problem. For example, Mrs M, whose own children had been experiencing a lot of bullying, said at the end of her group, 'Well, I still don't know what I'm going to do but I feel better'. The potential support of other carers can therefore work towards carers gaining emotional identification, sympathy and warmth, reducing the isolation which they often feel, giving encouragement, reassurance and very importantly validation of feelings such as frustration, anger and joy. (Such support is not necessarily confined to the meetings of the group. Usually because of relationships developed during the group sessions, informal networks and relationships also develop, so that carers will 'phone or visit each other or seek each other's help at particular times of stress.)

Though most schemes have social workers who maintain contact at an individual level, nevertheless there are a range of reasons, besides those already outlined, why such groups are also necessary. For a start, few social workers in generic departments are trained sufficiently in working with foster parents. They may also lack the experience of parenting themselves, which deprives them of status and credibility in the eyes of the carers. Social workers also on occasion can be seen as advocates for the child, preaching understanding and acceptance of what is at times seen as unacceptable behaviour. Support groups, however, are meant to complement individual efforts and not to replace them. A support group, for example, cannot provide the historical context of a child's behaviour, or a detailed analysis and consideration of everybody's point of view and of the family as a whole. Detailed planning, linking the ideas of parents, carers and children cannot be set out in support groups. Furthermore, having more than one source of potential support seems to increase many carers' confidence to take on and/or persevere with a challenge.

Our own observations and those of others running similar groups give strong support to the view that most adults when faced with difficult tasks and decisions tend to value the advice and validation of their peers. Because they all provide a similar service and face similar issues, they can more easily understand. As a source of support this does not involve a loss of face. Similarly, issues of confidentiality which may prevent carers from sharing possible difficulties with neighbours and friends do not arise. Some of the young people, for example, are adept at showing an acceptable face outside the home whilst being very difficult inside. Furthermore, group theory suggests that people are more likely to discuss difficulties in a group rather than in one-to-one situations, provided that the atmosphere is one of safety and of controlled intimacy where acceptance by the group encourages participants to share. The support group we run also tries to generate a sense of 'belongingness' or what Hazel (1981) describes as creating 'an artificial tribe.' In the long run a kind of corporate identity may be developed with participants identifying with the scheme and with each other. Such an identity reduces the sense of isolation, especially at times when there is a crisis or when things go wrong and a breakdown occurs. The celebration of social occasions forges feelings of 'oneness' and of informal mutual assistance outside the group. For example, it has been known for a carer to find a job for a young person living with another carer or to offer short periods of respite care to relieve a hard-pressed carer. Inevitably, such a group becomes increasingly powerful and in a stronger position to negotiate for better terms of work or for improved resources for their charges. In fact, the carers' own combined efforts may at times prove more effective in bringing about policy changes than those of social workers.

Learning takes place in both formal and informal ways. Much of the informal learning comes about through specific situations, e.g. 'How do I help a promiscuous girl?', or 'What can I do about his stealing?' Sometimes a comment made as a response to a problem can put things in a different perspective. For example, Mr L's response that perhaps 'we all really expected too much, we wanted the kids to change too quickly' (which is a frequent issue for carers) helped to look at the issue from another perspective. Issues such as these may have been discussed during the pre-placement preparatory sessions, but then they were hypothetical compared to the current actual experience. Not surprisingly preparatory input is better integrated after the carers have the experience of caring. Carers raise issues about the child as he or she is with them, as opposed to how he/she was described to them prior to the placement. Whilst some children turn out to be the way they were described prior to the placement, others can exhibit different behaviours or no problems at all, possibly as a result of the new family's dynamics and patterns of interaction. With time carers come to understand the information provided on a child better whilst also being more aware of their own strengths and limitations. In contrast, new carers tend to expect greater certainty than can be provided.

A frequent focal point for discussion in the group is the probable impact of past residential living experience on the children. The vast majority of children in my scheme have been in residential care for an average of 15 months. As a result they sometimes express surprise that the rules and expectations in a family can be quite different. Carers also tend to see the children as lacking in initiative and limited in their ability to make social links outside the home. The young people may equally feel uncomfortable about the degree of closeness present in the family which may also be expected of them. Those referring the children to the scheme sometimes underestimate these problems because they have only observed the child in the institution. This is in contrast to a minority of children who appear 'to sink into' a family and quickly find their niche there. Group members then describe them as having 'just fitted in' but this is usually the exception with the kind of children we place.

Other children may be worse in their behaviour, partly because of the reasons noted above, but also because for many, joining a family may cause a resurgence of feelings to do with their family of origin, and can provoke acting-out behaviour. It is like lifting the lid off feelings which have been suppressed for some time. If a child believes, as many do, that they are in care because they were 'bad', then a new family by welcoming them raises questions in their minds as to why this family likes, or at least tolerates them, when their own family did not or will not.

Processes

In the early stages of the group's life there is a tendency for those who present problems and issues to direct them at the group leader, which makes it difficult for the rest to help or support. It is part of the function of leadership to resist individual responses and encourage member participation. It usually takes some time before group members feel comfortable or confident enough to respond. In the meantime the leader tries to keep the discussion going without taking over. It is also not unusual for members to raise early on, intractable issues to which the group cannot immediately respond. The group may feel paralyzed, but the presenter may interpret this as lack of interest. As confidence increases, members begin to respond by commenting, offering suggestions, giving advice, encouraging or reassuring.

The following is a typical example. Mrs L. brought up an issue concerning John, who was 15½ and had been with them for about nine months:

'Well, it is just that John, you know he is so silly sometimes. He is just like a little boy. He giggles, behind his hand. And the other night he was leaning out of the window and shouting 'nostrils' at anybody walking past. And if I try to talk to him he giggles and turns his face away. He just does silly things. I don't know what he will be like at work or when he leaves the school.'

Mr T, one of the members, asked if John was like this at school. Mrs L. thought that John was OK at school, but very quiet according to the teacher: 'but I have to get on to him all the time in the house'. Mr T again:

'What do you mean about stupid things in the house?'

Mrs L: 'We can hear him if he is in the kitchen and he is giggling 'nostrils, nostrils', (laughs) and he just eats everything that is there like a big carton of ice-cream, one litre, in an evening. But he never puts on any weight! He is really skinny. That is all he does, eats and watches television.'

Another member then asked whether John had any friends. It turned out that John was a 'scared' boy who went very quiet if anyone he had not met before visited. I then asked what it was that Mrs L was worried most about.

Mrs L: 'Well, I do have to get on to him, like the other day it was raining, actually it was sleet, and he wanted to go out in his little bomber jacket and it took me ten minutes to get him to put his anorak on. I am always having to be on to him. But shouting out of the window at people, he shouldn't really . . .'

Another member then intervened to remark 'that she had a somewhat similar problem with Alec and he would make her nag at him'. She went on: 'But then I thought, well we are here to teach them right from wrong and I was lucky, Alec, he never bore a grudge, he just took a telling but I know it is rotten because you to have to be on to them.' Further exchanges followed from this:

Mrs S: 'I don't think you should feel bad, Anna, I mean I know you do but . . .'

Mr T: 'Aye, that is our job, you have to do it.'

Mrs L: 'But you know he is so silly and when he goes to work he's not really changed that much.'

Mr T: 'But you know you have got to be doing that and showing him what is right.'

Mrs S: 'But I know what Anna means, because when Steven first came I was always on to him about his washing and his table manners and, oh, lots of things and I felt bad so I know how you feel.'

Mrs L: 'Yes, but we still have to get on to him for so many things, I mean, well, we can put up with it but . . . he will leave school in a year and I don't know if he has changed that much.' (Pause).

Group Leader: 'You mentioned a couple of times what is going to happen to John when he gets to 16.'

Mrs L: 'He is very immature and I don't think . . . he is still very immature he doesn't listen, and you have to tell him and tell him and he still does not do it.'

Group Leader: 'It sounds as if you think you are not getting very far with him?'

Mrs L: 'Well we don't seem to.' (Pause)

Group Leader: 'Have other people had similar experiences?'

Mr C: 'Well, with Anne she did not seem to take anything in but now she will say things, now that she has left and it is things I said to her about saving money for the bills and so on. But it is hard.'

Mrs L: 'Maybe.'

Mrs McB: 'Sometimes you feel like you are just banging your head off a brick wall!'

Group Leader: 'So feeling frustrated and as if you are getting nowhere and maybe you are not doing a good job is something that Community Carers go through? My guess is that if you go back to the original referral papers and read them closely and remember how John was earlier in the placement you will find a lot of things you have achieved.'

Mrs L: 'Aye, I suppose so, yes okay.'

The carer's frustration, isolation and worry about the child's behaviour and future elicited support in the form of a shared problem and even some reassurances. Ventilating a feeling may sometimes be all that a carer is seeking and, more important, the knowledge that others understand. At other times there may be expectations for more direct assistance, in the form of suggestions. A further dimension is that at times the group may respond to the presenting problem failing to grasp the hidden message 'are we doing alright?' The need for recognition and reassurance cannot be underestimated. Many carers want to hear whether they are getting anywhere with a child and whether their approach seems also to others as sensible and appropriate. For example

Mrs B wondered whether they were getting anywhere with their child, 'because we are still having to check him for the same behaviour we were checking him for nine months ago'.

At other times a presenter of a problem may express this hidden agenda only obliquely and because of anxiety as to what the response might be. Not surprisingly the group may then have difficulty in picking up the anxiety. Mr C told a story of how a child had gone home for two weeks and he was unsure as to how to handle her when she returned. This was an important issue for him, but he was also experiencing a high degree of worry as to what was actually happening to the child at home. In such instances the tendency is to let the group run on but then confront it with issues it may have missed. In the case of Mr C this allowed a great explosion of worry which elicited a great deal of understanding and support.

As one might expect from such a group, a major issue for members is that of risk and security. The *raison d'être* for creating such a group is the expectation that it will stimulate beneficial processes of peer-group support and help develop new coping mechanisms. However, the approval and validation by peers also involves risks for the presenter: 'What if the group disapproves of what I have done? Can I share my difficulties?' Such an example is the group member who suddenly raises a major issue at the end of a meeting. Members may start by raising what they suggest is a minor point for clarification and as this is being discussed suddenly they raise a major problem-solving issue. Other members may find it altogether difficult to share difficulties until they have evidence that they are not the only ones experiencing them. A particularly difficult situation is sharing views about the breakdown of a placement. Breakdowns can be devastating not only for the child but also for the carers and their families. The need for both support and analysis of the issues cannot be sidestepped. The group leader has an obvious responsibility to create an atmosphere which will reduce inhibitions and anxieties, making it safe for members to share both negative and positive happenings. Informality, a warm and tolerant atmosphere as well as encouragement, need not preclude facing the group with possible difficult issues.

Leadership issues

It is a moot point whether such groups need to have a leader from among the professional staff on the scheme, or whether a leader should emerge from the ranks of the carers. Though the eventual aim is for the group to become much more autonomous, with the social worker serving it as a consultant, this has not yet been achieved. Currently the group leader, apart from arranging the meetings, assists members in drawing up a list of priorities or agenda for each meeting for discussion. Once this happens, he takes more of a back-seat role concerned with maintaining the group's task, providing direction to the discussion and occasionally giving factual information. Because of the danger of such a group over-concentrating on problems, there is a conscious effort by the leadership to encourage members to talk also about placements that go or ended well. The coffee break is another opportunity for such discussion. Talking about successes can, of course, be frustrating to some and give rise to feelings of envy among those who are going through hard times, but the situation is sometimes reversed at another meeting. Though group members are supportive towards each other, and can give praise, a real 'pat on the back' is expected to come from the group leader. This could be viewed as patronizing and stressing continued dependence on 'experts', but many members come to the group because they also expect some recognition and even appreciation for what they do. If professional social workers feel the need for appreciation, this is even more so for those involved in a 24-hour caring task. Perhaps group members will eventually become more spontaneous and less inhibited in giving and obtaining more open support. There is a similar reluctance to be on occasions more challenging and critical to each other.

SUMMARY

Support groups for community carers are a relatively new phenomenon not yet conceptualized in any great detail. They appear to fit within the 'educational' range of groups, but clearly their content and purpose are more personal than a simple group discussion. Many of the processes involved and observed are common to those of group consultation involving support and problem-solving. Though an educational or training element is retained, the group is decidedly supportive in nature. What support groups do is to highlight some of the issues which are concerned with group supervision/consultation by peers. They are fairly complex and demanding on both group leaders and members. For the group leader there are continuing complex decisions about how the group is functioning, its dynamics and its move from dependence to independence. There are also the dangers of destructive peer group power or of the group falling flat or never getting going, or that it may fall into maladaptive patterns.

From our experience gained so far, we have no doubts about the benefits of a support group to its members. Hazel (1981, p. 47) called them the 'keystone of the scheme'. They offer the opportunity for the creation of a peer group providing support and validation and new learning for individuals. They help to deepen the participants' sense of identity as community carers, and therefore to sustain them through difficult periods. In addition, participant carers provide an enormous pool of knowledge of parenting and, over time, experience of community caring which can be utilized for the benefit of individuals, including new carers who require help with problem-solving and support.

12

Foster parent support group in a rural area

Jana Brown

The main aim of this chapter is to describe the organization and structure of post-placement support groups for foster parents in a rural area, and also to identify some of the practice concepts and considerations that inform the running of these groups.

It is now recognized that post-placement groupwork with foster parents is not only desirable but necessary if foster parents are to be helped to care for the children placed in their homes. Very little has been written so far about foster parent support groups, particularly in the rural areas like the ones described here. As Crowley (1982) points out, most attention has been given to training and preparation groups, including those for specialist foster parents or community carers.

The development of a number of specialist fostering schemes in the 1970s has had a ripple effect on all forms of fostering. Fostering is now increasingly viewed as a many-sided activity, more diversified and with clearer definitions of tasks (Cooper 1978). As a result of these developments, the 'traditional' and 'exclusive' form of fostering practised in rural areas has also undergone a number of changes during the past decade. For example, foster families have gradually come to accept the fact that they not only provide love and a home to a child in need, but also that the fostering activity is a form of therapy for some of the children. As a result, they now view it as a task with its own rewards, but which also requires training, preparation and continued support after placement.

We have been running and supporting foster parent groups in South Norfolk for nearly a decade now. The evolution of the groups reflects new trends in foster care, the changing needs of foster parents and the way that the agency is trying to meet them. South Norfolk is the largest Social Services geographical area in the county and has a population of about 98,000. It is a mixture of semi-urban and rural settlements, mainly scattered villages and hamlets, with Norwich as a focus for most activities. The area covers approximately 350 square miles. The resources are scattered widely throughout, with the furthest point of the area being about 30 miles from the centre, with sometimes just one bus a week to Norwich. We have consistently had about 60–70 registered foster homes in the area and the percentage of children boarded out with substitute families is one of the highest in the country – currently 62 per cent. The enthusiasm for foster home care is steady, although the difficulties of home finding for the over 12 year-olds continues to be problematic.

The post of the area-based fostering officer was created in 1979 in recognition of the fact that fostering services needed to develop, be served and supported in a more consistent and professional way than was done previously. South Norfolk because of its rural nature is traditionally a supply, rather than a demand area for fostering resources, and tends to have a number of foster families approved but not fostering. The city is the demand area, and its social workers tend to look for resources in or around the city for easy access. There is a wealth of fostering resources to be tapped in these areas, although the trend has been towards the traditional fostering of younger children, and towards fostering as a multi-purpose activity. This is not surprising as the local community resources for adolescents are limited. There is also some apprehensiveness among families with younger children about fostering older ones where the need is greatest.

This situation inevitably leads to part of the fostering resources being under-used. We have always been conscious of the fact that if we do not keep the interest of foster families alive in other ways than by placing a child, we would lose a great number of foster homes before we were able to make a placement with them. Foster parents who feel that they are not needed become uninterested and are lost.

The rationale for the groups and their organization

In a rural area, where the fostering resources are scattered around and not readily accessible for frequent individual visits, the forum of a foster parent group can fulfil several purposes from the fostering officer's point of view. We can have regular monthly meetings with fostering or non-fostering families, monitor the placements that are ongoing, keep readily in touch with changes in the foster families, or can use the attendance or continual absences of previously regular members as an indication of problems, uninterest, animosity towards

161

the Department, satisfaction with the *status quo* or what you will. Non-attendance usually does express something and can then be followed up by an individual visit.

The existence of foster parent groups is not, as the previous paragraph may suggest, for the convenience of the fostering officer. We believe that post-placement group supportive services to foster parents are essential because individual, on average three-monthly, visits are not enough. While the term 'support' can mean several things, in this context it is helping foster parents in the task of taking children into their families and providing the appropriate service for the child, the natural family and the local authority. For example, Jones' (1975) study of foster parents who ceased to foster showed that 40 per cent did so after one year, and one of the main reasons causing this was insufficient support. Foster parents were let go, where they might have continued as foster parents had more support been available to them.

Traditionally, support to foster parents is provided by the agency worker, in this case a fostering officer. However, it was thought that the foster parents would benefit far more if this task was shared by other foster parents. Most rural foster parents are isolated in their fostering activities and there may not be another foster family for miles. By exchanging information about the problems that a placement may be producing, offering and receiving advice, sharing the experiences, the joys and the sorrows of the placement, the group members would feel far less isolated in their role. The provision of support to existing foster parents, as well as keeping alive the interest of those families who are not currently fostering, was originally the main reason behind establishing three such groups in South Norfolk. The invitations to group members were based on geography, not on the specific fostering task undertaken. My personal involvement is in the group based in a small market town. Its membership originally consisted of experienced and new foster parents fostering on a short-term basis. Monthly invitations are sent to about 15 families, but the core of the group regularly attending is about eight, either as couples or singles. Those foster parents who were fostering a child on a long-term basis were reluctant to join the group, perhaps feeling that the child was so much part of the family that the term 'fostering' no longer applied to them. They did not feel the need to belong to a group, and thought that their contribution to it was perhaps irrelevant, a point also made by other writers.

From the beginning of the groups' operation we have always involved new applicants who were either considering fostering or were being individually assessed. The group very much welcome the new faces and rises to the task of initiating the newcomers, feeling they have a place in preparing and training new applicants for the task. They relish imparting the most off-putting experiences they have had with their foster children, and enjoy watching the expressions of amazement, embarrassment, respect and surprise on the applicants' faces. They are also interested in who the new applicants are, and always enquire how their applications are proceeding. The willingness of the established members to include the new members, to share their experiences, and the desire to help them, has always been a marked advantage of this group.

Since the group has always included a small number of foster parents who are not fostering, the latter's attendance at the group helps to bridge the waiting period and keeps the interest alive. These foster parents can see that they are not unique or in some way penalized by not having a foster child, since there are other people in the same position. It must be said, however, that if a placement is not made for a long period of time, even the most attractive foster parent group cannot fill the vacuum. As a result, the would-be foster parents stop attending the group since they no longer see themselves as having the status of a foster parent. Worse still is the feeling that they cannot contribute to the group and therefore have no place in it.

The development of a 'linked' fostering scheme over three years ago (i.e., a time-limited 'professional' fostering scheme concentrating on the assessment of adolescents in foster homes) has produced 'specialist' foster parents. The tasks of the latter are clearly defined, the financial rewards are greater and their status is different. The inclusion of the three 'linked' couples in the group gave it a more dynamic orientation and more awareness of the departmental needs. Although the 'linked' foster parents have the advantage of attending a group specifically designed to meet their needs, they continue to come to this group because of geographical convenience. It was inevitable that after nearly ten years the fostering functions of the members of this group would change. Short-term foster parents become long-term ones, long-term foster parents may adopt the child they have been fostering, and some foster parents become 'linked'.

Because the group has always been versatile, and not specifically orientated towards a particular type of fostering, it serves a multiplicity of purposes and its members can select what they get out of it. This was particularly seen when members who stopped attending because they felt the group was no longer meeting their needs with a particular child, or that they did not need the group, returned to it when a different child arrived. The easy-going and welcoming atmosphere of the group enables them to return, feeling that the group is stable enough to meet some familiar faces again and also that it is interested enough to hear about their new child, or about a difficulty.

In a rural community, where the foster parent group serves a wide range of foster parents with different tasks, the risks are obvious. The domination at one time of one sub-group with one specific task over another can easily upset the balance. The shift of concentration on, for instance, a small section of prospective adoptive parents over a period of time, would mean loss of interest for, say 'linked' foster parents. Our experiences have shown that the group has to be flexible and wide enough to meet the different needs. It cannot do this for all members at all times, and perhaps setting up a separate group with a specific orientation would be more appropriate. However, by keeping the membership as wide as possible, and by encouraging the cross-fertilization of ideas and experiences, this group has been beneficial to both new and established members. Members themselves find comfort in the stability of the group, and are resistant to drastic changes.

Content and process

As already stated, support to foster parents and peer support has always been the main purpose for establishing a foster parent group. The fostering officer, as a leader and the one constant attender, provides not only continuity at the monthly meetings but also information, contributes to problem solving and acts as advocate and link person on behalf of foster parents vis-a-vis the agency. New developments in the fostering scene country wide, the trends in foster care, the level of demand for fostering resources. etc., always receive a great deal of interest and are demanded. The inclusion of the 'linked' foster parents who, because of their involvement with other groups, tend to be better informed and more aware of the pertinent issues, has meant that the content of the monthly meetings is more widely based, the group is less insular and the leadership more shared.

With the rising awareness of foster parents and the different and more difficult expectations placed on them, the inclusion of continued training in the group's activities is inevitable. Though most foster parents have been through the 'Parenting Plus' training course, its influence, as Crawley (1982) found, appears to lessen with time. The ongoing support group with its elements of training, information giving, exchange of views and the mutual support it offers, continues and keeps alive the fostering as a parenting plus activity. For example, as part of continued training, sessions were provided on drug abuse, family therapy, sexual abuse and other topical issues. The group responds to the 'training' element of the sessions and occasionally asks for the same speaker or topic to be repeated after a period of time. For instance, a talk by the Drug Squad three years ago was interesting, but when repeated recently many foster parents had actually experienced the problem and were asking for guidance on detection, symptoms and treatment. Other talks are arranged on such topics as new research into adoption versus fostering, juvenile delinquency, access law and regulations, and life story books, or are given by speakers from residential establishments.

Most of the group's time, though, is taken up in discussing the basic essentials of the fostering task, including the management of emotional or behavioural problems, or of parental visits and contacts. One topic discussed at a recent meeting concerned the wish of an 11 year-old girl to change all her names. The group considered how advisable this was, why she felt like this, the impact of such a move on the small rural community, the reaction of the natural family, etc. Bed-wetting and the frustration of trying to cure it, adoption versus custodianship, and how former foster children are progressing are some other topics discussed recently. Almost every meeting discusses the social workers and their performance. Foster parents are quick to praise 'good' practice and equally condemn what they consider as 'poor' practices. The fostering officer present has not infrequently been put on the spot.

The rejection of a foster mother by a foster child usually provokes a lot of discussion. Such a problem arose recently in one of the foster families. The child not only returned the Christmas presents but blamed the foster mother for his terminal illness, which was most upsetting to the foster family. The group were very sympathetic and supportive. Advice was also offered on how best the foster parents could respond to this behaviour. The fact that the foster parents are able to talk about issues and problems such as these in a forum where others, although not experiencing them, understand the dilemmas and the difficulties is mostly experienced as supportive. There are few people that the foster parents can truly talk to about rejection, stealing, lying or other problems without appearing to be failing in their role as foster parents. With increasing confidence and trust, they are able to do so in the group.

Support is not a tangible thing, it is felt by the group members, rather than consciously given by others. Nodding of heads, expressions of sympathy, 'it must be difficult for you', 'I don't think I could cope with that', 'how do you manage?', etc., all fall into the category of support. Outright advice is not often given, although similar experiences and how they were coped with are recounted. Equally rare is direct challenge, and perhaps the group could have done with a little more. Disagreement with an opinion or a way of handling a particular problem tends to manifest itself in the interchange of looks, silence, immediate change of topic, loss of interest or perhaps the expression of disagreement to the leader in private. The group usually has one or two couples who are not in tune with the rest in their ways of thinking, attitudes to child care, or what are seen as 'acceptable' ways of dealing with problems. These foster parents tend to leave the group after a while as it does not meet their needs and they do not feel at ease with the other members. We have not yet found ways of holding them.

Because of the turnover of foster children, different dimensions of the same problem can be presented and foster parents can observe that the same handling does not always yield similar results with different children. The discussion around actual children and behaviours is particularly welcome to new applicants present. Foster parents get to know each others' foster children, their peculiarities and problems and get or give sympathetic and supportive response or share in problem-solving. Overall, group members seem to value the meetings with all their elements of support, information giving, training and problem-solving. The group is structured enough to be goal and task-orientated but with enough informality to encourage trust, sharing and, increasingly, risk-taking. Out of these meetings have also evolved friendship and social acquaintances without turning the group into a social gathering. The agency itself would have had no interest in such a group.

However, the organized traditional Christmas party given for foster parents is something the latter look forward to. The social workers from the area are invited, which helps to promote communication between the two groups, and it is also an opportunity for the agency to thank the foster parents for their work and commitment. This is extended to another social gathering in the summer, usually in the home of one of the members, which is very informal. People enjoy seeing each other's homes which seems to contribute to the easy-going, friendly atmosphere that permeates the meetings throughout the year. Several friendships have evolved as a result of meeting on a regular basis, of people who have seemingly nothing else in common but the fact that they are fostering children.

Boundaries

One issue which has in the past received some attention in the foster care literature is how to keep the focus of the discussions between social worker and foster parent on the fostering task, and not encroach on the boundaries of the foster parents' own family. The boundaries are easier to observe when the problem is unrelated to the presence of the foster child, and members do not bring to the group what are personal matters. However, foster parents, not infrequently, refer to the impact of the foster child on their own children. This is also something new foster parents want to know more about. Most foster parents then describe this impact as beneficial. Occasionally though, it is said that an own child 'cannot stand' a foster child.

Generally, the meetings are orientated to foster children and not natural children. Foster parents mention the reactions of their own children only in passing, unless there are grave problems. For example, in one case the foster placement was breaking down due to the adverse reaction of the natural children – regression at school over a period of time, resentment of the foster child and continual complaints about his behaviour, attention seeking, disturbed sleep, refusal to relate to the foster child in any way, withdrawal from parents. This was discussed over a period of time, but only in relation to the foster child, not the other way round. In another instance, the foster child involved the natural children in theft. Although the children's loyalty was to the foster child initially, on discovery by the parents this turned to resentment and rejection of the child. Great discussions ensued. One set of 'linked' foster parents decided to stop fostering teenagers as their own boys were entering adolescence. The foster parents felt that they no longer wished to expose their children to the sort of behaviour that the youngsters in care display. In retrospect these foster parents felt that their children were adversely affected by the continual change of the foster children. Once the family stopped fostering, the children became much more outgoing and the relationship with the parents became closer and more trusting.

Leadership issues

The question of leadership has been discussed periodically as the eventual aim for the group was to become self-supporting. When the group is functioning, seemingly effortlessly, the membership is steady, the sessions are dynamic and the foster parents have a dialogue with the agency through the individual visits and the Foster Care Association, it is repeatedly suggested that the fostering officer may well withdraw. This always meets with a great deal of resistance by the members claiming that the group would disappear. The foster parents go as far as to suggest that the withdrawal of the fostering officer from the group would constitute abandonment by the agency. The fostering officer has always taken an active role in running the group and is not allowed to be passive by its members. This is partly due to the new applicants for whom the fostering officer is the only familiar face and all communication is directed to her, and partly to the fact that an agency leader can prevent a clique or a sub-group from taking over and keep the group functioning on a consistent theme.

The group leader has a crucial role in channelling the discussion, involving the individual members and, if necessary, dampening the enthusiasm of others. The group's functioning is periodically threatened by one or two members, whose contribution may seem irrelevant or repetitious. Consequently, after they are continually challenged about their views, they begin to feel isolated and find the group threatening. The fostering officer, as the leader, finds herself in the unenviable situation of having to keep members' interest alive whilst also keeping the more repetitious contributions to a minimum. She has to bear in mind that if not given the space, the group will not meet the need of those foster parents who obviously need a great deal of support (and will eventually withdraw without the group being able to help them modify or, indeed, look afresh at their attitude and opinions).

In rural areas where people live in scattered communities, where travelling is a problem and people may lead fairly isolated lives, the foster parents can be reticent in wanting to be involved in any kind of group activity. The foster parent group has to be made very attractive to justify making the necessary effort to attend. Unlike the time-limited, sharply focused 'Parenting Plus' course, or preparation groups, which demand a concentrated attendance for a few evenings, this group is ongoing and requires more continuous effort. The pattern of meetings we adopted was to alternate the open meetings with more sharply focused sessions with either a speaker or a video on a particular topic. A very fine balance of organized activities needs to be achieved in such a mixed group. The group members are usually unspecific about who or what they wish to have at the meetings. They tend to place the responsibility for the organization and the running of the group fairly and squarely on the agency. Such dependency may appear unhealthy, but experience has shown us that any variation in the location, the day of the meeting or temporary leadership, is too threatening and detrimental to the group.

When the attendance falls, one sure way of boosting it is by hiring a video-tape which will be of as great interest to as wide a number of people as possible. On one occasion when we showed the video on incest counselling, the initial response was as expected and half as many more people attended than usual. Consequently, the group was too large and fragmented and resembled a conference.

Although we would wish for most foster parents to be involved in a support group, we may have to think about establishing another forum for those who are more inclined to respond to a direct input, and perhaps feel more comfortable in a more structured, educative, possibly time-limited group.

Reflections and evaluation

This group has now been functioning for nearly ten years and continues to thrive with the occasional drop in membership, but it is always a viable forum with a stable core of members to meet the needs of rural foster parents. From the foster parents' point of view, the benefits of attending the support group are several. It gives them a sense of belonging and a certain status. Fostering in rural areas is an isolated and insular activity. There may not be another foster family for miles. Foster parents from different walks of life and varied lifestyles have a common ground, however widely it is based. They welcome the opportunity to share experiences and views with each other. It gives them insight into similar problems which they experience and they draw upon the different and combined experiences of the group members. This helps to overcome isolation and frustration and to find comfort in the knowledge that difficulties are common in fostering and not peculiar to themselves or to their foster children. Foster parents whose placement ended in disruption, use the group to air feelings of frustration, sadness, guilt or dismay. They equally feel more able to voice possible dissatisfaction and anger with the agency in a more forceful manner than they are able to do to the agency worker.

Because of the knowledge of each others' fostering activities, one of the advantages of the group is the fact that on a few occasions they are, with the agency's agreement, able to provide for each other holiday or weekend relief when it is appropriate. Due also to the fact that the group is a mixture of foster parents with different fostering interests and functions, we are on occasions able to transfer a child from a short-term placement with a family attending the group to a long-term placement, also with a family from the group. Consequently, the transition is often easier and less painful for the child and for both families.

For the purposes of this chapter a simple questionnaire was circulated to the members to try to evaluate the reasons for their attendance, and to ascertain what they most valued about the group. For the majority of the members, the main reasons they gave for attending the group were those of sharing with others their problems and difficulties, giving and obtaining support, and finally that they enjoy it.

Company, friendship and help were the main gains for the members of the group. The relative isolation of the foster families in the rural areas is obviously partially alleviated for those members who feel it most acutely. The original purpose of setting up the group continues to remain the same. Any attempt on our part to change it overtly towards, say, more training, or give it more structure, is likely to meet with resistance.

Listening to foster parents' experiences, rather than participating, was reported to be the most enjoyable thing about the group for most participants. Equally enjoyable were the special talks given by speakers, which may suggest that the participants see others rather than themselves as making the group enjoyable for them. In contrast to an earlier reply, when they said that they came to the group to share, the subsequent answers suggest that they enjoy getting rather than giving.

The most valued thing for the participants is apparently the contact with other foster parents and with the fostering officer. The contact with the agency representative must be high on the list of priorities, as half of the members would only 'possibly' attend the group if the fostering officer was not present, and the other half would not attend at all. It seems that the leader in this context is seen as enabling the members to benefit from and enjoy the group, and is seen as the force behind the continuous functioning of this group. No one member was willing to take over the running of the group, the main reason being the reluctance to relinquish the link and liaison with the agency. The interest and willingness of the agency to support its foster parents via this forum is extremely valued, and withdrawal of its resources would not only affect the group's functioning, but might well result in a much more fragmented and dissatisfied fostering service.

SUMMARY

It has already been stated that, although the value of discussion groups for foster parents is widely recognized, not all foster parents are interested in joining or participating in any form of training. In the rural areas this is further complicated by the geographical distance, and there is, in addition, no firm expectation that new foster parents or prospective applicants will participate in a group activity. However, making the group attractive by a rolling programme of open and structured meetings, with a stable, if changing membership, and by building-in the social gatherings and promoting informality and friendship, the group can attract and maintain its momentum. Whether attendance at a support foster parent group influences attitudes and performance compared with non-attendance is still an open question. My own view is that attendance at post-placement support groups may not influence the outcome of a fostering situation, but it does help foster parents to cope with it while it lasts.

13

An independent adopters' support group

Sandra Hutton

This account expresses my view as a member of the Lothian Adopters' Group (LAG) and describes the organization of the group.

LAG was started in 1982 by adopters in Lothian Region who were keen to help the Social Work Department in recruiting new families by describing some of their experiences to prospective adopters. However, the main function of the group soon became one of support as we reflected on what was happening to us and exchanged views on how to cope with the difficult behaviour of our adopted children, most of whom were placed as 'special needs' children having some degree of emotional handicap.

By its formal constitution, LAG is accountable to its members although to help the group carry out some key functions the Social Work Department has funded the post of the LAG Secretary and also funds the costs of running sub-groups, and payment of fees for counselling by LAG members and other support activities. The recognition of the need for the service provided by LAG and its active encouragement by the Adoption Unit in Lothian were significant in the evolution of the group.

Initially, the growth of LAG was slow but gradually an increasing number of us – adopters and also long-term foster parents – came forward to admit to needing such a forum. By late 1986 LAG was servicing about 120 families and new adopters are automatically encouraged to take advantage of the network provided by LAG. Agencies involved in adoption are also offered group membership and access for their families.

At first the establishment of our group was seen as a challenge to some of the professionals. Gradually, however, relationships with social workers which had been conducted on traditional professional/client lines have been superseded by an increased partnership. Some workers who did not like this new way of working and possibly saw us as a threat, ceased to be identified with the group in any meaningful way. Recent adopters however know no other methods or approach and are often surprised how radically the practice in Lothian has changed over only a few years, while stories from the recent past have already taken on the hue of folklore.

The newsletter and monthly meetings

Monthly meetings continue to be an important forum for many of us and regular contact with all members is maintained by post, including a monthly newsletter reporting on meetings and organizational developments. The newsletter also floats suggestions, and ideas and experiences which are considered potentially helpful to our peers are recounted. We see the newsletter as both informative and supportive.

It was when we were able to express some of our fears and failings in the newsletter that we stopped being a flag-waving band of successes and were released to relate to each other in a much more meaningful way. After this the depth of the worry we all carry began to be apparent and to be acknowledged in our contacts with each other. We can find that it is a great relief to know that it is acceptable to speak of difficulties or concerns without fear of being judged as failures. The pooling of the experiences of so many families is a marvellous opportunity to learn, and the knowledge and respect which we individually acquire in the group helps to rebuild our typically vulnerable self-esteem. The supporting services are also able to learn a lot from our sharing.

After a number of newsletters had been issued we extracted from them a list of serious concerns which were subsequently used as agenda for monthly meetings. These included coping with a range of the children's behaviour, issues about their past experiences and our concern for their futures, professional help and practical resources. Often we discuss these matters ourselves but sometimes we invite outside experts to lead the discussion.

Sharing and mutual support

To become adopters of older children many of us had to persevere and even insist to prove how capable we are. When we reached the limit of our capability the shift from our aggressive independence to asking for help was very painful. The links afforded by the group allowed us to discover that we are not alone in this feeling and to overcome our reluctance to seek support. There seems to be a direct relationship between our willingness to share and our ability to use the help offered by the network. Over time, as we keep in touch with others, we see people we have come to respect getting every bit as tired and perplexed as ourselves. Then it is much easier to admit to our fellow adopters that all is not well for ourselves either and to seek appropriate help. Much of that help we get from our peer group but all of us need more from time to time.

Involvement with the group is an ongoing commitment for some, but most adopters tend to move in and out of the network as it suits them. We certainly do not discourage the more casual approach and we are glad that members who can dispense with LAG for a long time still feel free to return when they need additional support.

The initial admission of needing help may seem brave but the barriers were broken out of desperation. Having set such a pattern though, we like to think that we have made it easier for new adopters to ask for help quickly and without loss of face.

The preparation group

Inevitably our attitudes to seeking help and joining peer support groups were partly influenced by our initial selection and preparation group experiences. The composition and function of the preparatory group introduced and established a number of ideas for us as adopters. One of these was the idea of partnership and joint working between social workers and adopters expressed in the involvement of adopters as co-leaders. We learned that adopters who experienced groups led solely by social workers found themselves challenging the professionals' communications and statements, sometimes discounting them as having sprung from cynicism, or even ignorance. There seemed then to have been a gap in communication between the two groups. Later on, when we adopters as co-leaders gave an equally hard and uncompromising message about what was involved, we too found ourselves under attack and our credibility questioned. Trying to convince the uninitiated of what we know through experience, and their resistance to receive or accept the message can give rise to frustration on both sides.

It seems that for many of us, until the reality of caring for special needs children is experienced, statements about possible future difficulties are resisted. Potential adopters get considerable reassurance at preparation groups where they meet people who have already had children placed with them. However, they continue to be sceptical when we try to put across the message, based on experience, that many problems, far from receding after placement, are likely to increase and may even be compounded. We are aware that families seem reluctant to take this message on board, as indeed we were ourselves. Couples with their own children also assume, when listening to difficulties, that their tried parenting skills will prove equally effective with their adopted children. Later they feel perplexed that these are not successful. It is probably necessary for would-be adopters to start with an over-optimistic, if not idealistic view about human nature, otherwise none of us would have embarked on adoption at all. Adoption of special needs children, particularly older ones, is about hopefulness, yet this contributes to the difficulties in acknowledging the presence of a problem and seeking help.

Group members generally appreciate and value seeing social workers and adopters working on the same task. Traditional models of authority are replaced by roles which implicitly convey acceptance, respect and joint working. It has not always been this way. Some of us remember when we approached the Social Work Department, cap in hand, and would accept almost any inconsiderateness to achieve our goal. The process generated some bad feeling which still colours some of the reactions of our members. As adopters of special needs children we want to be seen, not as clients requiring management for inadequacy, but as people offering our abilities to provide a family for children who need it, whilst also satisfying some of our own needs.

Long-term support

The setting up of post-placement support groups is a recognition that problems may shift and change but also continue for years, perhaps indefinitely. In retrospect some of us wish we had understood this better, not because it would have essentially changed anything, but it would have helped us to prepare better and to face the long-term strains with less surprise and anguish. Perhaps adopters going through the preparation groups today with the opportunity of meeting families years into placement, with steady social work contact, post-placement group participation and a network of peers, start off from a much more realistic and informed base.

Sub-groups

When we began we were a group who had had our children for some time. When others joined us they were in the first flush of enthusiasm and high energy. Though it is good for us to meet at different stages of the post-placement period and for initial keenness to meet more measured commitment, the groups can also be dominated by the heavy end of experience.

In recognition of this imbalance and also to cope with the growing numbers in LAG, we decided to divide LAG into various smaller groups to enable more exchange between members at similar stages but still continued to hold meetings which provide a general forum.

The larger group has now quite naturally split into three and it is possible broadly to identify our problems by the groups we belong to. Whilst our wish and perhaps temptation is to want to hand down our hard-won lessons, especially to the newcomers, we are all limited in that kind of learning and it is in the intimacy of our own peer group that we really sort out where we are and what we are going to do. It is a feature of our meetings that we make maximum use of time. No matter what subject we start with we very soon come back to basics – our relationships with our children and issues of discipline and care. We generally avoid seeking social occasions though private friendships develop.

Early placement group

The first LAG group comprises newly formed families or families still waiting for a placement. For all of us the waiting period is particularly difficult. Membership of the group can allay the limbo feeling to some extent and it is perhaps the best way of keeping alive the idea that a placement will be made. The families already in placement are usually lively with the cut and thrust of getting to know each other and as some problems are beginning to emerge, seeking tentative solutions. It is probably true to say that this group is vigorously engaged with problem solving and is rich in invention and success. Common themes discussed include lying, feeding problems such as overeating or food hoarding, and the need for discipline. This is when it is often acknowledged that such parenting is hard and the need for movement constant. Some courageous statements also emerge such as 'we thought it would be hard but not this hard'.

As already stated, a considerable amount of the group's time is taken up in talking about behaviour, such as eating habits, which can assume large proportions. For example when one couple ventured their worry about finding food hoarded in the child's room they felt relief on hearing of similar experiences from other couples. Equally there is relief in hearing about situations which we too have experienced with shame or humiliation. We may then discuss our anxiety about the deeper significance we sense in problems acted out over superficially trivial issues like food, clothes, etc. and can progress to make suggestions about at least finding ways of dealing with the behaviour.

Another theme which recurs in the early placement group is the theme of manipulating behaviour. One example is the child who communicates with only one parent and excludes the other from any satisfactory relationship, giving rise to envy and friction. The group has no ready-made solutions but we can explore the feelings. In this kind of example some of the group may ask how each parent reacts; others may criticize the loyalty of the spouse who readily receives the child's attention at the expense of the marital relationship; or again others may question whether it is the child's attitude to his natural parents which now governs his way of attachment to his new parents.

The group struggles to find explanations and make suggestions. It is difficult to know how to define these processes other than as a form of group counselling and group support.

The middle group

Some of us in the middle group are in a stage of real crisis around two years after placement. We are struck with the realization that our children have suffered damage of irreparable depth. We have become more conscious of what we cannot achieve and our mourning of the 'lost years' before we knew our children causes further pain. It is difficult to accept that when our children suffered damage we were not there to prevent it. Instead we begin to understand that the improvements in our skills cannot heal what has happened in the past. Then we understand that our children's innate potential can never be realized to the extent which we had previously expected. Consequently, we sense a futility about the extraordinary energy we have expended on problem-solving and are left quite uncertain of how to proceed.

There is some comfort in grieving with others rather than alone and we tend to support each other against the outside world. At this time of crisis much of our talk is about how little we are understood by those around us, even those close to us over other life issues. The message from outside that we are merely experiencing what any family goes through becomes less tolerable and sometimes only other members of the group can convincingly support our defence against this pernicious half-truth. We finally begin to part with our hopeful picture of ever being like the families who insist on telling us that we are like them, if somewhat less successful.

Perhaps we get little understanding from outside because the change is in our appreciation but not in our circumstances. Even when we think we understand this we still have no good reply to such comments from others as 'I told you so' and 'you knew what you were taking on'. However, one reassurance within LAG comes from hearing adopters who also have natural children and who can invariably describe the vast difference they find in their adopted children. Even those who have long experience as parents are not meeting with the success which they had expected in their bid to make someone else's child part of their natural family.

Advanced parenting group

Four years of placement can produce another, deeper crisis. What are we to do with the knowledge that our children are irreparably damaged and not even our high determination can repair and make good? Probably we return with renewed energy to the problem-solving and are likely to be engaging professional outside help as a protest against the enormity of our realization. We may decide to tackle afresh a behaviour problem and base our hopes on life improving if only such behaviour can be pushed underground. When such a burst of energy fails to take us back to the hopefulness of our start, we are in crisis indeed. The only change that is going to be effective now is change that comes from our children and that is now painfully unconnected to the effort we put in ourselves.

In partnership with the social workers a number of families in this third group have been engaged over the year in a course called 'Advanced Parenting Skills'. The gains of this course have been considerable for discussion and exploration of issues and behaviour. For example, one of the themes which occupied the group is sexuality and how we form our ideas and attitudes on the subject. Inevitably this led to disclosures by members of behaviours by their children and how they reacted to them. For instance, what appeared to some members as over-reaction by the parents over an incident with sexual connotations, to the parents themselves felt much more alarming because of its apparent lack of precedent or connection with anything they had been aware of.

What may appear to outsiders as superficial or small incidents can awaken all kinds of insecurity and fears in us as parents. There is a tendency then to begin to attribute current behaviour to the past experiences of the children.

This fear of the unknown input in the past causes us colossal loss of confidence in our children.

Loss and further separation

Common to all sub-groups within LAG is a preoccupation with loss experiences in the past and present and the prospect of separation in the future. These concerns may emerge in any of the groups and loss is a subject which we have grappled with at the monthly meetings also.

If we are parenting a child from a failed adoption, it is helpful to share with others who have that experience too. Our concern can be that if our children will not be forthcoming about their past experiences this may stand in the way of the development of a deeper relationship.

However, we have been so overwhelmed by our awareness of our children's losses that it may be some time before we realize the extent of some of our own losses as parents, whether loss of liberty, loss of conventional acceptance, loss of our early optimism or loss of the opportunity to bear our own children. Childlessness especially can preoccupy many of us and the therapeutic value of the group is in acknowledging that pain and loss. One example was the disclosure by one of us that her inconsolable feeling of loss as a childless mother was triggered by the birth of an unplanned late child in her wider family. The group responded sympathetically and silently to her sadness, meeting that sadness in a unique way.

In searching for and discussing new skills to cope with the intractable, most particularly in the advanced parenting skills group, we have come to understand together that such a search has a limited outcome – a conclusion which seemed most unlikely at the beginning of the course. We have disclosed the deep disappointment we all feel because of what we realize will never be achieved. This is yet another loss. Knowing that there are parts of our children which belong to other people is quite different from what we might have been prepared for – that parts of our children cannot belong to us. It could be said that we are faced with two choices in beginning to live with this major change. We can look for ways beyond what we personally can offer to help our children to move on, if they can, though psychiatric help or group therapy with other adopted children. We can also give ourselves permission to re-route our energies into other areas of life and accept that our wish to change the unchangeable may once again have to be met in other ways. We are much more likely to achieve a positive outcome if we are given group support in this process of letting go. Not only are we letting go of our never-to-be-realized pictures of our children but we are also letting go of our idealized pictures of ourselves. That can add up to quite a shattering package and we are unlikely to get the acceptance and understanding we need anywhere else but from our peers.

Our support group would not be worth much if it were for winners only and perhaps it can be said that being in such a group gives us permission at any stage to achieve less than we would have strived for. For some of us the letting-go process may mean parting from our children. If the feeling of being stuck is overwhelming, then separation may be the most comfortable resolution. Older adoption is about change and if we reach a point where change is no longer possible, then ending may be the only way forward. If we look at adoption as a journey with our children which is essentially their journey, then we must not expect to be able to control the route they have to take. We may make a bid to change that route but at the end of the day we have to accept that we may be quite far short of our desired destinations.

Practical support services

Because of the special needs of our emotionally handicapped children our members see the need for a range of practical services, not dissimilar to those required by non-adoptive parents who have to cope with more obvious handicaps. These include: respite care to cover unaccompanied holidays for the children; regular breaks – perhaps one weekend every month; and crisis relief. There is a similar need for financial underpinning, possibly in the form of adoption allowances to contribute to such costs as: damaged clothes and possessions; extra educational tuition; supervised recreation; sports and music tuition; and providing socialising opportunities for the children. Some of the children, because of their history, do not easily fit into existing groups and require separate arrangements.

SUMMARY

It is my view that post-adoption support must be organized by adopters and backed up by a specialist team of social workers and other professionals to service it. The post-support groups have highlighted both the need and value of peer support and equally exposed our frailty. Joining the group is a kind of admission of needing help, something that for those of us who thought of ourselves as copers felt awful and an admission of failure. Our newsletter, monthly meetings, discussions and counselling, outside speakers, professional advice and practical services, help us to face the challenge.

Those of us who have suffered the anguish of disruption equally want to be sustained by our fellow adopters with whom we have shared the good and the bad times. Then we can begin to move from a preoccupation with the distress of disruption to gradual withdrawal from the group to a new form of normality without our adopted child. It is important to stress the spirit of optimism and co-operation that exists in the group and the fellowship between adopters from vastly different backgrounds who have been brought together by common circumstances. While LAG members have little inclination to indulge in social activities for their own sake, LAG itself is a successful social group which reminds us that we as parents are just as important as our children and indeed that our success as parents depends on our having an adequate quality of life. This quality of life is possible only if we can achieve a measure of separation from our children, something all parents need. At its simplest, the single factor we can identify which marks our parenting as special is that we are attempting the contrary prime objectives of attachment and separation almost simultaneously, or at best unnaturally close together.

Over the first five years since LAG was established our understanding of and views about the children, ourselves and the adoption service have undergone many changes, each change being tested by the experience of many others as we learn from each other. The key has been to accept such changes and indeed to anticipate that there will be more. On one point we are all agreed – the best way of supporting our children is for us adopters to receive the best possible support from our adoption agency, from other support services and from each other.

14

Groupwork with transracial foster parents

Audrey Mullender

The limitations of an individual approach to training and support

A number of authors have identified the issues on which prospective white foster parents of black children should receive training. Pryce (1974, p. 384) thought that white foster parents should be briefed on cultural issues and also prepared 'for some of the shocks and stresses they will encounter in bringing up a black child in a generally discriminating and race-conscious society'. The National Foster Care Association (NFCA, undated), recognizes factors to be covered in preparation concerning black cultures and also the need to try and understand the experience of racism. ABSWAP (1983, p. 11) extends its concerns from training into the selection of new foster parents and, not unnaturally, takes a wide-ranging stance covering all the areas for which transracial placements have been criticized (see above, Chapter 10). The Association believes that the family and the black child should have black friends and other contacts in the black community, and that the family should give the child a positive sense of its ancestral past and religious background and of multi-racial society including race relations problems. The attitudes of other children of the family, the extended family, and neighbours are seen as very important and, overall, the child must be helped to develop a black personality through being accepted 'as a black child in a positive way' by prospective carers who have shown that they can '"work through" their conscious or unconscious feelings of threat from blacks' (ABSWAP, 1983, p. 11).

The limitations of work with prospective foster parents, in relation to the problems of transracial placements, are summed up by this optimistic remark in the House of Commons Social Services Committee's Second Report (1984, p. cxxii): 'What is needed to overcome those problems is appropriate support for such placements, so that foster-parents, children and social workers are aware in advance of possible conflicts and are as equipped as they can be to deal with them as and when they arise.' The key words here are 'in advance'. Even assuming that practice does improve to the point where this high level of preparation and maintenance could be attained, it would still do nothing for those placements which were made some while in the past, before the particular difficulties of placing black children in white families were realized, let alone surmounted.

Cheetham (1981, pp. 49-50) within the British element of her Anglo-American comparison of services, draws together the issues both of preparation of new foster parents and measures which can be used to improve existing placements. Unfortunately, other than one or two more active authorities (Cheetham, 1981, p. 73), she found a bleak picture in relation both to prospective and current foster and adoptive parents: 'There were hardly any attempts to combat the short-comings of transracial placements, for example through special preparation for substitute parents or through liaison with local black people. The few black "uncle and aunt" schemes were not pursued with much vigour' (Cheetham, 1981, pp. 49-50). Cheetham is, of course, well able to say later in the report what she believes white substitute parents should be able to offer black children placed with them, including relevant books, historical and cultural information, actual contacts with black people both individually and through organizations, and open discussion of the all-pervasive racial discrimination (Cheetham, 1981, p. 73). However, it seems likely that only what I would call the 'converted', that is, those who already recognize the failings of the previous 'colour-blind' or 'colour is only skin deep' approaches, will be attempting to give their black children these positive experiences. Payne (1983) probably did locate relatively 'converted' transracial adopters in her small-scale study since she contacted them through Parent to Parent Information on Adoption Services, an information service with a self-selected take-up. Thus, although what they told her they have attempted by way of activities and attitudes towards their black children is not entirely reassuring, it is at least a beginning:

> 'We listen with them to black music, we buy books and comb the library for books with black children. They have black and white dolls.' 'We also deliberately encourage friendship with other black children, and have one or two friends of negro origin.' 'If there is anything about the child's country in the newspaper we show it to him.' Other parents wrote of plaiting hair with beads and encouraging daughters to make the most of their curly hair and pretty, dark skin (Payne, 1983, p. 21).

The 'converted' will not only see the problem, but try to discover what to do about it; for example, in Liverpool, white foster parents have 'sought black "godparents" or "guardians" for the children in their care', a scheme which is said to have worked well (Smith, R., 1985, p. 4).

Attempts to spread good practice beyond the few 'converted' include efforts by local and national foster parent organizations to educate and train their members. For example, NFCA (undated leaflet) as well as encouraging foster parents individually to gather information from the local black community and its resources, also offers a range of ideas on people and places which local groups can list as useful contacts or with whom they can set up networks, perhaps through the local Community Relations Council. National bodies mentioned include the Commonwealth Institute, the Commission for Racial Equality and the Africa Centre. As in assessing children's needs, however, the only way to ensure coverage of every transracial foster placement is to have a comprehensive, authority-wide policy. Small (1985, p. 11) addressing a day conference on transracial fostering and adoption in Nottinghamshire advocated this in place of an *ad hoc* approach:

> You need to take on board the issue of providing some sort of structure for white families fostering black children . . . linking the families with black people, with black organisations; providing resources for them to get books that have black people in positive situations . . . because this society, the TV, the press, radio, are always reflecting the positive aspects of white society and the negative aspects of black people.

The same authority that has introduced new and universal review responsibilities in relation to individual children in transracial placements, that is Bradford, has also introduced complete coverage in distributing separate notes of guidance for caretakers of Afro-Caribbean children and for Asian children (Mennell, 1986, pp. 122-3). These are very thorough and spell out numerous ways in which individual foster parents can meet their foster children's needs, including through contact with the extended family and with voluntary, religious, and cultural organizations, 'provision of [specific] papers, magazines, posters, clothing, television and radio programmes, music', plus video films for Asian children, and through meeting practical needs for special hair and skin care, or language, or particular foods. Issuing notes in this way is an improvement on leaving advice-giving to individual social workers, or simply waiting for foster parents to spot the issues themselves, since many in both groups may be unaware of what is needed and what is available. It also recognizes the responsibility of the care authority in supporting and educating its foster parents rather than appearing to blame them for being unaware that views on transracial placements have moved on considerably since their black foster children were placed with them. Notes of guidance can reach everyone but, nevertheless, there is no guarantee that all social workers and foster parents involved in transracial placements will read, digest or make any use of the guidance offered in the notes. Above all, it is not a method which is likely to change the attitudes of those who do not believe such special measures are necessary. Thus Mennell reports (1986, pp. 125-7) that a minority of staff were not willing to consider the racial dimension or to seek support and information; that a small number of fieldwork staff and carers had colluded in allowing some children to pass as white, and that practical help was much more widely accepted than was the idea of actually contacting black people through, for example, black organizations.

The next section will introduce groupwork with transracial foster parents and adopters as potentially a more effective way of reaching beyond the improvement of their practical knowledge to their feelings and attitudes.

A groupwork approach with white foster parents of black children during established placements

Background: The possibility of using groups instead of an individual approach to follow-up work with substitute parents, after transracial placements have been made, is not a new idea in the field of adoption. Kreech (1982, p. 119) and Raynor (1970, pp. 189-90) give brief accounts of discussion groups in the USA and in Britain respectively. The members of the groups in both countries picked out issues of their black children's racial identity and heritage and Raynor, in addition to areas common to any adoption, mentions that the groups were interested in their children's experience of racial prejudice. Both authors describe groups with essentially educational and supportive functions and Raynor (1970, p. 190) emphasizes that this, though a positive experience, cannot amount to fundamental re-education of someone who should not have adopted in the first place. Whilst this is true, it is unclear how far these groups challenged unhelpful attitudes or racially prejudiced views in their members or in wider society. White's more recent study of a few transracial adopters, whilst it does not cover groupwork, does touch on the discovery that horizons of understanding can be widened to a marked extent by discussion with others in a similar situation:

> All the couples except one believed that black children have no different needs from white children . . . The couple who believed their mixed parentage child had special needs had only recently arrived at this viewpoint from conversations with adoptive parents of black adolescents. They now emphasized the need to cultivate positive self-identity in the child. To do this efforts early on were felt to be necessary in order to counteract racism (White, 1985, p. 10).

More deep-seated attitude change, in relation both to adoption and fostering, is seen as necessary by ABSWAP (1983, p. 11), evidently with a group setting in mind: 'White families who are currently fostering or who have adopted a black child should be given race awareness training. These training sessions could be conducted along the lines of pre-adoptive and foster care classes.' The whole section on 'Transracial placements – a good practice guide' (ABSWAP, 1983, pp. 10-12), which contains the points raised earlier in relation to selection, is 'in note form with focal areas which', states ABSWAP, 'should be useful for topic focus training of transracial adopters' and, by extension, foster parents. Reaching approved transracial foster parents to invite or require them to attend groups would normally be easier than offering post-placement support to adopters, since foster parents retain contact automatically with the placement agency. Both groups could benefit from a groupwork approach to the sort of areas highlighted by ABSWAP, however.

The Ebony Foster Parent Group: The Ebony project, established by Nottinghamshire Social Services Department, consists of a group for young black people in white foster homes which has run on two occasions (the second of which was described in an earlier chapter) and a further parallel group for the young people's white foster parents which has run once to date. In both group settings, there is an attempt to raise the whole range of issues in relation to transracial placements, including practical, cultural, racial and identity material. Thus the workers running the foster parent group set goals which combined Kreech's and Raynor's educational and supportive groupwork model with the ABSWAP idea of reaching deeper attitudes.

The detailed aims of the foster parent group were:
1. to provide opportunities for white foster parents of black children to share experiences, problematic or otherwise;

2. to act as a training resource covering aspects of physical and emotional needs, including the question of racial identity;
3. to try and enable the foster parents to develop a culturally aware parenting style towards the black children for whom they were caring;
4. to offer foster parents a model of the survival skills which a black child needs in this society.

Overall, it was hoped:

> to educate white foster parents and help them to dispel their colour-blind attitude to black children in care and to realize these children have different needs. It is not enough to give black children love, warmth and security but that these children become strong black individuals. We also aim to help white parents address their own racial stereotypes and attitudes, and to learn to find ways of bringing black cultures into the care which they offer to black children (Thorn, Skerritt, Smith and McGlade, 1985, p. 5).

The first issue which the leaders of the foster parent group had to tackle was that of resistance amongst the group members. Unlike the young people's group, which was marked by an eagerness to participate at a range of levels, the foster parent groups was essentially defensive in atmosphere initially. No doubt the foster parents were only too well aware of the current climate of criticisms of transracial placements: perhaps they felt that they too were inevitably under criticism. They may even have feared that if they revealed too much of themselves or of any difficulties they might be experiencing, their children could be at risk of being moved. The potential for foster parents to feel threatened has been recognized ever since the first Ebony young people's group was planned, as Miller (1985, p. 18) stresses:

> before the group sessions commenced, the group leaders acknowledged the love and care that these children were already receiving. This group was not designed to undermine the transracial placement, but to enable the black child to realize that he or she is black and to learn to use this in a positive way.

Consequently, referrals to all the Ebony project groups have been made by the children's own social workers, not by specialist workers from the black fostering project who could perhaps have been seen as 'invading' the foster families with dangerous new notions. Despite this safeguard, the suspicions of white foster parents, in any project like this, that their placements may be coming under threat should not be underestimated, especially in view of the public's confusion about further transracial

187

placements on the one hand (together with the more recent backlash, see for example: *Community Care*, 10 July 1986, p. 3; *Childright*, July/August 1986, p. 5; and comments in the House of Commons Social Services Committee Second Report, 1984, p. cxxii), and, on the other hand, the question of plans for existing placements, about which far less has been said. Small (1985, p. 11) was alert to the probability of this element of confusion and to the consequent fears of foster parents, when he addressed a social workers' day conference in Nottinghamshire less than ten days before Ebony ran for the second time:

> I am not here to say that my intention or the intention of where I work, is to pull out the black children that are currently in white families. There are situations where I would agree as an Assistant Director to do that, but after a very firm and clear assessment of what is happening, and very clear evidence of disorders and very clear indicators that this family is unlikely to be able to continue to provide care for these children. It has never been the intention of my Authority, or myself, to withdraw black children from white families where they have been placed and I think I need to make that absolutely clear . . . Now our white foster parents and adoptive parents are going through a very difficult period, a period fraught with anxiety about the attitudes of blacks towards them. Social Services Departments have got an obligation to provide some sort of structure to enable these families to be sensitized to some of the issues that people like myself are talking about at present.

Ebony can provide this kind of structure, but must clearly be aware of the sort of concerns foster parents may feel when asked to join an Ebony-style group.

Transracial foster parents may fear even the process of being 'sensitized' to issues, to use Small's phrase, if they see this as likely to alienate them from their black foster children. For example, 'Many white parents may feel reluctant to go too deeply into such discussions [that is, about blackness, self-worth, and racism] with their adoptive or fostered black children because of a fear of distancing themselves from the children whom they fear may possibly feel resentment against them should their black consciousness be developed' (Children's Legal Centre, 1985, p. 7). Others may be apprehensive in case they become too associated in their foster children's minds with the pain of having to confront unresolved emotions. This was one of the major reasons why the Ebony young people's and foster parents' groups were planned in parallel and around very similar material. It was felt that by encouraging development in both sets of participants around similar issues at the same time, it would be possible to dispel some of the myths held by foster parents (or indeed the children, or their social workers), that differences in awareness, or a growing black identity and confidence on the children's part, would lead to the disruption of placements. In response to an expectation of all these concerns amongst white foster parents, and of their possibly stereotyped view, even, that all black social workers would be somehow 'against' them, the foster parent group had a mixed leadership of two black workers and one white.

Most members of the group clearly displayed their anxieties as to how they as transracial foster parents were seen, through their unspoken but transparent reactions to the group itself: 'Initially, all except one of the foster parents saw the request that they and the children attend the Ebony Group sessions as a criticism of their ability to care for the children' (Nottinghamshire Social Services' Department (hereafter Notts. S.S.D.) 1986, p. 16). Since they felt their quality of parenting was under scrutiny, they were also worried about what their foster child or children might be saying in the young people's group, which was meeting at the same time in an adjacent room. The decision to hold two distinct groups for the young people and their foster parents had been taken after careful thought by the joint leadership team of both groups. It was based 'on the need for the work with the children to be suitable for their level of understanding and to allow them the freedom to explain how it felt to be on the receiving end of colour prejudice, without feeling disloyal or fear[ing] hurting their foster parents' feelings' (Notts. S.S.D., 1986, p. 16). The compromise of holding both groups in the same building on the same evening was struck in order to ease travel arrangements but the report on the groups acknowledges: 'The separation of the groups contributed towards the foster parents' feelings of anxiety about the intentions of the Ebony Group. Most were concerned about what was happening in the other group and their inability to control this' (Notts. S.S.D. 1986, p. 17). This must have been particularly frustrating at times when the sounds of fun and laughter came from the games being played in the young people's group.

The content of the material used in the foster parents' group did not entirely reassure its members either. A similar differentiation between topics which registered as 'safe' and 'less safe' was noticed, as was recorded in individual work by Mennell (1986, p. 126): 'There was a far greater acceptance of the need to concentrate on practical issues such as hair and skin care than to confront racial issues, attitudes and stereotyping.' Not surprisingly, in the already uneasy atmosphere of the foster parents' group, some areas were found to be particularly sensitive:

> One of the primary aims of working with the foster parents as a separate group had been to enable the white foster parents to examine how best to help their black foster children to sustain their blackness. However, few of the foster parents were prepared, in the early stages, to consider looking at this element of their care of the children. They were more than happy to discuss their concerns and needs regarding hair and skin care but were hesitant to look at the possibility of differing methods of child care and/or parenting skills, or the need for them to learn about aspects of black culture and history as a means of helping the children (Notts. S.S.D., 1986, p. 16).

The foster parents appeared to have expected practical rather than emotional needs to be dealt with, and they were far more comfortable during sessions like the ones on West Indian cookery or on hairstyling. In order to avoid looking at the more painful emotional and racial issues, the foster parents would tend to deny that their foster children experienced the typical difficulties of black people, owing to their middle-class upbringing. They did not see their children's blackness as requiring special attention, thus displaying an individual version of the dangerous 'colour blind' approach, which Cheetham has placed in the wider context of childcare services, describing it as:

> usually based on fear of the acknowledgement of racial differences or the existence of a multi-racial society, a fear which may be a product of an individual's own barely recognized prejudices. In fact, many black children are disadvantaged precisely because no account is taken of their culture or appearance, and it is assumed that the most natural and proper way of conducting affairs is according to the norms of the majority white culture (Cheetham, 1986, p. 9).

The disadvantage suffered by the black foster children of these white foster parents was that the latter were: 'ill-equipped to help their black child to cope with society's prejudiced attitudes' (Notts. S.S.D., 1986, p. 16). Another form of rationalization used by the foster parents to avoid facing painful topics was to make comments such as 'We will cross that bridge when we come to it' or 'They are too young to understand' (Notts. S.S.D., 1986, p. 17), and other remarks to the effect that discussing their blackness with their foster children would only stir up the children's anxieties unnecessarily. These defences against discussion at a deeper level made the group extremely hard work for the leaders. They gently persisted, however, and:

> accepted that discussion about origin and culture may well cause stress or hurt to the child at times and emphasised that warmth, love and honesty and

really sharing sensitive issues would overcome stress or hurt. The benefits of this enabled the child to grow and develop and be more likely to become a well-adjusted person, better able to face the realities of what life can be like without the protection of the family (Notts. S.S.D., 1986, p. 17).

Further evidence of the painful nature of the group experience for many of the foster parents was their erratic attendance, together with the high drop-out rate. The core group dropped to a membership of only four or five. This no doubt also reflected the lack of awareness amongst some of the children's own social workers of the need for such a group, since not all of them stressed its value or encouraged the foster parents to keep going along when their enthusiasm flagged. On a more structured level, any department running such a group, whether for prospective or current foster parents, should consider making attendance a requirement since those least 'converted' to the content may also be the least likely to consider or to maintain membership of such a group.

As mentioned earlier, the content of the foster parents' group was very similar to that in the young people's group (which was described in more detail in Chapter 10 above), although different emphases naturally developed. The first session was planned identically for the two groups with an introduction to the group, and a video on racial prejudice. Over several sessions, the foster parents' group used a brainstorm technique to consider what the words 'black' and 'white' mean in everyday language and also to reflect on their meanings to those present. To illustrate, responses to the word 'white' included 'pure', 'clean', 'good', 'white magic', and to 'black' included 'dirty', 'bad', 'evil', 'trouble', 'blackmail', 'black mood', 'black cloud', 'black magic'. Stereotypes of white, Afro-Caribbean, and Asian people were also brainstormed and the assembled lists included the following words and phrases: 'white – superior, professions, dependable, ideal family, high I.Q'.'; 'Afro-Caribbean – sporty, deprived, riots, trouble, irresponsible'; 'Asian – money grabbers, illegal immigrants, Social Security scroungers, smelly'. Reasons behind the reactions to the brainstorm exercises were examined, as were suggestions as to how change might be achieved. The latter included: 'mix together more, education, use library and resources in area, learn about black history, ask people', a collection of pointers to improved care which compares favourably with those listed in the earlier section on individual approaches to tackling criticisms of transracial placements.

The foster parent group also had a practical session on hair and skin care, and one on West Indian cookery in which a meal was prepared. The two black group leaders discovered that they disagreed over how to prepare a certain dish which injected a lighter note into the atmosphere and also demonstrated, more generally, how diversified Caribbean culture is. The cookery session ended with a positive experience of sharing, when the foster parents, children, and group leaders ate the prepared meal together. A discussion on cultural awareness at another week's meeting, which included explanations of black family lifestyles, structures, behaviour, attitudes and values, revealed complete ignorance about extended families. The foster parents all agreed they had given the matter no thought, but could now see how easily they could have given offence, or misunderstood expectations of them. One example involved the custom that family members would all be expected to stay in one house together for wedding celebrations, no matter how over-crowded it became, and the fact that it would be impolite not to accept such an invitation. Similarities as well as differences of lifestyle were identified, and the session proved valuable in going some way towards achieving acceptance of different cultures. A session on the geography and history of the Caribbean revealed that the foster parents could name only a very few of the islands of the West Indies, and that many did not know where their foster child's family had originated.

As can be appreciated from the foregoing, the foster parents who did attend the group were at a very early stage in relation to confronting issues of different cultures, let alone of race and racism, since they had had no previous opportunity to participate in discussions of this type. Consequently, they found it difficult at first to relate the ideas presented to them to their own foster children's lives, especially as they had begun by putting a good deal of emotional energy into denying the existence of racism in society or its relevance to their foster children. The 'saving grace' of the group, in addition to the skill and persistence of the leaders, was the presence in the group of one more aware white foster parent who offered a great deal from her own experience. One of the most productive sessions was one centred on incidents of racial prejudice that foster parents had encountered or could imagine. Initially, the discussion 'stuck', with very little forthcoming except denials of the topic's relevance, until this particular foster mother offered evidence from her own foster daughter's experience. She showed that black adolescents are faced with inevitable racism, for example in being singled out for attention by the police, however unassuming and well-behaved they personally may be. Her anecdote 'freed' the other foster parents to be able to recognize potential areas of discrimination against young black people, such as in finding accommodation or employment, and in educational disadvantage. It was not clear, even then, whether they would truly believe in such instances of racial prejudice until they experienced them through their own foster children, and they certainly still felt that the Social Services Department should take on the responsibility for handling all these problems, rather than the foster family itself.

There is no doubt that eight weekly sessions gave only a very short total amount of time in which to confront the foster parents' lack of awareness of cultural and racial issues, combined with their denial of racism and high anxiety as to whether their own placements were threatened, or were at least under the spotlight of criticism. Future groups of this type would benefit from an extended length. Even so, the foster parents – by the end of the group's life – evaluated it positively. They felt they had benefited from it as a useful learning experience, had enjoyed airing their views and sharing experiences of similar situations and difficulties, and had appreciated the chance which Ebony gave them and their foster children to meet other transracial foster parents and children, especially as they had felt rather isolated before the group. The foster parents further considered that they had been given valuable practical advice, and that they had been challenged to think more deeply, thus developing a heightened awareness of their foster children's needs:

> The foster parents also appreciated the chance that the Ebony Group gave to their children to meet and mix with other black children. The benefits of this highlighted to the foster parents the needs of the children to socialise with the black community, especially as a way to enhance their sense of identity (Notts. S.S.D., 1986, p. 19).

By this stage, the group members' progress was demonstrated by their recognition of a previous lack of knowledge of their foster children's family backgrounds and their possible difficulties in forming relationships both with white people and with black, in the latter case for reasons which might include non-comprehension of dialect or of cultural differences. A number of the foster parents also demonstrated their newly-kindled wish to supplement their knowledge of racial and cultural issues by substantial purchases of books and other resource materials during the joint visit to the Commonwealth Institute after the foster parents' and young people's groups ended. It was the consensus of opinion at the end of the foster parents' group, that this type of opportunity for group-based discussion and learning should be available for all current and future transracial foster parents.

Alternative models of groupwork with white foster parents of black children

The chief difficulty encountered by the leaders of the Ebony foster parent group was the initial denial by the members that their black foster children had any special needs, accompanied by their resistance to admitting that ours is a racist society. In any future work of this kind, the Ebony project has confirmed that it is essential to hold separate group meetings for the foster parents and their foster children, since their perspectives are so different and their respective anxieties would severely inhibit one another. If reasons of budget, travel or other practicalities dictate that the two groups meet simultaneously in the same building, then they should be out of earshot, owing to the inevitable curiosity and apprehension about what the other group may be revealing, which can make the sound of the other group more fascinating than one's own.

Although the two groups would then be run separately, experience has shown that building in some joint activities is of great value. For example, the informality of the day trip to the Commonwealth Institute was a positive experience of sharing by the foster parents and their foster children in the context of learning about West Indian life and customs. In addition, the meal afterwards at a Caribbean restaurant was the third West Indian meal which the two groups had eaten together. The first was the product of the foster parents' cookery session and the second was a meal prepared by two of the leaders of the young people's group during a presentation by a guest speaker. Eating together works on several levels. It has symbolic significance (especially in a deeply Christian culture), over and above the practical element of learning new customs and transferring them into normal daily life. The basic idea of shared activities could be extended further into a joint period held routinely at the end of each group session when the young people and their foster parents could be helped to compare and reflect further on the material which their respective groups had covered, and the feelings and attitudes it had evoked.

Now that the level of foster parent resistance and discomfort can be predicted, it creates the opportunity to examine alternative ways of approaching groupwork with transracial foster parents. Firstly, increased individual preparation of the foster parents for the group, either by each child's social worker or by specialist fostering workers, could be used to 'explain its role as a purely educative one and a sharing of experiences, not as the foster parents having to pass yet another "test" as to [their] suitability to be foster parents' (Notts. S.S.D., 1986, p. 17). If sensitively and thoroughly accomplished, this pre-group work would go some way towards reassuring the foster parents that their quality of care is not being criticized and that their transracial placement is not in jeopardy. Rather, they will be coming along to a group to learn about what their black child is likely to meet in the wider world outside their loving, caring home. Using social workers beyond the group leadership to undertake this preparatory work would demand a high level of understanding in the social workers themselves. Those referring and preparing foster parents and children for the group, would need to agree fully and overtly with the group's educational, supportive and developmental goals and not, for example, to see it as a form of therapy to prescribe for families with relationship or other problems.

It might also be decided to extend the individual preparation of foster parents beyond explanation of the purpose of the group into some preliminary work on race issues, perhaps to the point of recognition that there is racial prejudice in society, so that foster parents are better able to go on to learn from an Ebony-style group about identity issues and survival skills, for example. Having reached that stage before the group started, they would be able to suggest things they wanted to work on in the group and the social worker undertaking preparatory work with them could also identify learning needs to help orientate potential members to what the group can offer. Social workers and foster parents may in future be given an information pack about the Ebony project before the referral stage, which will contain basic information such as venue and dates of the next group to be run, but also its aims, an outline of the proposed content, background information, and perhaps answers to probable unstated fears and myths about being invited to join the group.

In addition to increased preparation, a second recommended change for future foster parent Ebony groups would be to aim for a balance of 'aware' and 'less aware' white foster parents so that they could learn from one another and also challenge one another's assumptions and resistance. Alternatively, it would be possible to combine black and white foster parents in one group, although this could perhaps be experienced as threatening by the white foster parents. In fact, the foster parents who met as part of the Ebony project did request in their evaluation that input from black foster parents be built in to future such groups so, potentially, one or more sessions of that kind could be planned.

Whatever the composition of the group itself, the mixed leadership appeared to work well and gave the foster parents both black and white adults to whom they could relate. An alternative leadership team might include both social workers and aware foster parents to lessen any implication of 'instruction' by 'experts'. The present author joined the worker team of the foster parent group as consultant when the planning stages (jointly undertaken with the leaders of the parallel young people's group) had already been concluded. Serious attempts had been made up to that point to find black consultants for the two groups, but only one was forthcoming, so he worked with the all-black leadership of the young people's group. The lesson to be learnt from this is that any black groupworkers in projects like Ebony should see themselves, and be seen by colleagues, as potential consultants. Receiving good supervision and consultancy support themselves will help them to develop the necessary skills, and they will bring the crucial added dimension of their own black experience which I, as a white person, inevitably lacked.

Finally, it would be interesting to reflect on whether a less worker-led style of group might help to alter the tone of the foster parent group, and make it less resistant, in the same way that a more educational model has, in some agencies, replaced or supplemented the investigative approach to assessment and selection of adopters (and, by extension, foster parents) for children with special needs (Raynor, 1974, reporting on Kay Donley's methods at Spaulding for Children in the USA; Alton, 1981, reporting on Parents for Children). Alton (1981, p. 16) prefers the educational model because 'It more readily produces a trusting and open relationship between worker and adopter' which seemed to be what was initially lacking between workers and foster parents in the Ebony foster parent group. The educational approach is less likely to create defences than is the 'vetting' approach to selection because it is based on 'a genuine attempt to give adopters appropriate information on which to base their decision about what sort of child they are best able to parent' (Alton, 1981, p. 17). The link with Ebony might, for example, be that preparatory work preceding an Ebony group could be undertaken through an 'open' style of group meeting with experienced social workers, black foster parents and white transracial foster parents present to give information and answer questions. In their own time, and in a more relaxed way, foster parents who were new to the issues could apply the proffered material to their own circumstances, and decide which aspects they wanted to work on in any ensuing groupwork context. It could be that their defences would already be too strong to allow them to respond freely even to this more voluntary and uncommitted beginning, so that they still denied the existence of any areas they needed to work on. Alternatively, Alton's note (1981, p. 17) in relation to people who, after all, have not yet been approved as substitute parents, that 'basically the family is helping us towards a better knowledge of themselves in relation to a real child' could also be applied to foster parents who have already had one or more children placed over a period of years, and whose lack of 'awareness' about racial and cultural issues up to this point is as much their placing agency's responsibility as it is their own. Then, new information could be explored by agency workers and foster parents together, perhaps in joint training groups for white foster parents and white social workers, so that foster parents do not appear to be shouldering all the blame for their 'unaware' parenting in the past. A shared discovery of the potential for improved practice in existing transracial placements could be a fitting achievement for the Ebony project and an important sign of a more hopeful future for the many black children currently living in long-established white homes.

References

General Introduction, pp. 10-15

BALL, C.M., and BAILEY, J.G., 'A group of experienced foster parents', *Case Conference*, Vol. 15, No. 12, 1969, pp. 471-4.

BION, W.R., *Experiences in Groups*, Tavistock, 1961.

BROWN, A., CADDICK, B., GARDINER, M., and SLEEMAN, S., 'Towards a British model of groupwork', *British Journal of Social Work*, Vol. 12, No. 7, 1982.

DILLOW, L.B., 'The group process in adoptive home finding', in TOD, R., ed., *Social Work in Adoption*, Longman, 1971.

DOUGLAS, T., *Basic Groupwork*, Tavistock, 1978.

DOUGLAS, T., *Group Living*, Tavistock, 1986.

JONES, M., ed., *The Therapeutic Community – A New Treatment Method in Psychology*, Basic Books, 1953.

KIRK, D., *Shared Fate*, Collier-Macmillan, 1964.

KIRK, D., 'The Selection of Adopters' in *Medical Group Papers II: Genetic and Psychological Aspects of Adoption*, Association of British Adoption and Fostering Agencies, 1970.

LINDERMAN, E.C., 'Group Work and Education for Democracy', *Proceedings of the National Conference of Social Work*, Columbia University Press, 1939, pp. 342-7.

MCWHINNIE, A., 'Group counselling with adoptive families', *Case Conference*, vol. 14, no. 11, 1968, pp. 407-12, and vol. 14, no. 12, 1968, pp. 456-8.

MILLS, R.B., SANDLE, R.R. and SHER, M.A., 'Introducing foster mother training groups in a voluntary child welfare agency', *Child Welfare*, vol. 46, no. 10, 1967, pp. 575-80.

PETERSON, J.B., and STURGIES, C.H., 'Groupwork with adolescents' in SCHWARTZ, W. and ZALBA, S.R., eds., *The Practice of Group Work*, Columbia University Press, 1971.

RICHMOND, M., 'Some next steps in social treatment', *Proceedings of the National Conference of Social Work*, University of Chicago Press, 1920.

SCHULMAN, L., 'Programs in Groupwork', in SCHWARTZ, W. and ZALBA, S.R., eds., *The Practice of Group Work*, Columbia University Press, 1971.

SCHWARTZ, W., 'On the use of groups in social work practice', in SCHWARTZ, W. and ZALBA, S.R., eds., *The Practice of Group Work*, Columbia University Press, 1971.

SLAVSON, S.R., *The Fields of Group Psychotherapy*, John Wiley & Son, 1956.

STANLEY, R.L., 'The group method in foster home studies', in *Social Work Practice, Report of the 20th Annual Forum Conference in Social Welfare*, Cleveland, Ohio, 1963.

WALTON, H., *Small Group Psychotherapy*, Penguin, 1971.

WATSON, K.W. and BOVERMAN, H., 'Pre-adolescent foster children in group discussion', in TOD, R., ed., *Social Work in Foster Care*, Longman, 1971.

Chapter 1, pp. 19-26

BECKFORD INQUIRY, *A Child in Trust*, Social Service Dept., Brent, London, 1986.

BERRIDGE, D., and CLEAVER, H., *A Study of Fostering Breakdowns*, Dartington Social Research Unit, 1986.

BOYD, L.H. and REMY, L.L., 'Foster parents who stay licensed and the role of training', *Journal of Social Service Research*, 2, Summer 1979, pp. 373-87.

BRADLEY, T., *An Exploration of Caseworkers' Perceptions of Adoptive Applicants*, Child Welfare League of America, 1966.

CAUTLEY, R.W., *New Foster Parents*, Human Sciences Press, 1980.

COHEN, J.S., 'Adoption breakdowns with older children' in SACHDE, P., ed., *Adoption: Current Issues and Trends*, Butterworth, 1984.

CROWLEY, M., *Preparation for Foster Care Practice: A survey*, Social Work Monographs, U.E.A. Norwich, 1982.

GOODACRE, L., *Adoption Policy and Practice*, Allen and Unwin, 1966.

HAZEL, N., *A Bridge to Independence*, Blackwell, 1981.

HAMPSON, R., 'Foster Parent Training' in COX, M.J. and COX, R.D., eds., *Foster Care*, Ablex Publishing Co., 1985.

JARRETT, J.M., and COPHER, M.W., 'Five couples look at adoption', *Children Today*, vol. 9, no. 4, 1980, pp. 12-15.

KAGAN, R.M., and REID, W.J., 'Critical factors in the adoption of emotionally disturbed children', *Child Welfare*, vol. XLV, no. 1 (February) 1986, pp. 63-73.

KIRK, D., *Shared Fate*, Collier-Macmillan, 1964.

KIRK, D., 'The selection of adopters' in *Medical Group Papers II: Genetic and Psychological Aspects of Adoption*, Association of British Adoption and Fostering Agencies, 1970.

LAHTI, J., 'A follow-up study of foster children in permanent placements', *Social Science Review* 56, 1982, pp. 556-71.

MACASKILL, C., *Against the Odds: Adopting Mentally Handicapped Children*, BAAF, 1984.

PARADISE, R., and DANIELS, R., 'Group Composition as a Treatment Tool with Children' in BERNSTEIN, S., ed., *Further Explorations in Groups*, Bookstall Publications, London, 1972.

REDDY, W.B., 'Sensitivity Training or Group Psychotherapy; the need for adequate screening', *International Journal of Group Psychotherapy* 20, 1977, pp. 366-71.

SIMON, R.D., and SIMON, D.K., 'The effect of foster parent selection and training on service delivery', *Child Welfare*, vol. LXI, no. 5, 1982, pp. 515-24.

SMITH, P.B., 'Introduction', in SMITH, P.B., ed., *Small Groups and Personal Change*, Methuen, 1974.

Chapter 2, pp. 27-39

BARKER, R. and HUTCHINGS, J., 'A Training Course for Foster Parents', *Adoption and Fostering*, vol. 5, no. 4, 1981, pp. 25-8.

BASTIAN, P. and ODAMS, M., 'Foster Parent Training in Calderdale', *Adoption and Fostering*, vol. 7, no. 2, 1983, pp. 19-22.

BRUNTON, L. and WELCH, M., 'White Agency, Black Community', *Adoption and Fostering*, vol. 7, no. 2, 1983, pp. 16-18.

DAVIS, S., MORRIS, B., and THORN, J., 'Task Centred Assessment for Foster Parents', *Adoption and Fostering*, vol. 8, no. 4, 1984, pp. 33-7.

DOUGLAS, T., *Groupwork Practice*, London, Tavistock, 1976.

HORNE, J., 'Groupwork with Prospective Adopters', in SAWBRIDGE, P., ed., *Parents for Children*, British Agencies for Adoption and Fostering, London, 1983, pp. 8-13.

PARFIT, J., *Group Work with Parents in Special Circumstances*, National Children's Bureau, London, 1971.

SCHROEDER, H., 'Black Applicants to Ealing Recruitment Campaign', *Adoption and Fostering*, vol. 9, no. 2, 1985, pp. 50-3.

SMALL, J.W., 'New Black Families', *Adoption and Fostering*, vol. 6, no. 3, 1982, pp. 35-9.

SMITH, P.B., *Group Processes and Personal Change*, Harper and Row, London, 1980.

TUCKMAN, B.W., 'Developmental Sequences in Small Groups', *Psychological Bulletin*, no. 63, 1965, pp. 384-99.

Chapter 3, pp. 40-56

BERTCHER, S. and MAPLE, R., *Creating Groups*, Sage, 1977.

CARTWRIGHT, D., ed., *Studies in Social Power*, Institute for Social Research, 1967.

HARTMAN, A., *Finding Families*, Sage Publications, London, 1979.

KIRK, D., *Shared Fate*, Collier-Macmillan, 1964.

KIRK, D., 'The Selection of adopters' in *Medical Group Papers II: Genetic and Psychological Aspects of Adoption*, Association of British Adoption and Fostering Agencies, 1970.

LIEBERMAN, M.A., YALOM, I.D. and MILES, M.B., *Encounter Groups*, Basic Books, 1973.

MCKAY, M., 'Planning for permanent placement', *Adoption and Fostering*, vol. 99, no. 1, 1980, pp. 19-20.

MORRISON, J.C., *A Tool for Christmas*, Church of Scotland, 1981.

SATIR, V., *Conjoint Family Therapy*, Science and Behaviour Books, 1967.

SATIR, V., *People Making*, Souvenir Press, 1970.

SIMON, S.B., *Values Clarification – A Handbook of Practical Strategies for Teachers and Students*, Hart Publishing Co., 1972.

SMITH, P.B., *Group Processes and Personal Change*, Harper and Row, 1980.

Chapter 4, pp. 57-68

CHESHIRE FAMILY PLACEMENT SCHEME, see account in *Community Care*, Dec. 1982.

CROWLEY, M., 'Preparation for foster care practice', *Adoption and Fostering*, vol. 6, no. 4, 1982, pp. 48-50.

HAZEL, N., and COX, R., *The Special Family Placement Project. Progress Report for 1975*, Maidstone: Kent Social Services Department, 1976.

LONDON BOROUGHS REGIONAL PLANNING COMMITTEE, *Survey of Special Schemes in London*, 1982.

MCWHINNIE, A., 'Professional fostering', *Adoption and Fostering*, vol. 93, no. 3, 1978, pp. 32-40.

NATIONAL FOSTER CARE ASSOCIATION, *Education and Welfare in Foster Care*, NFCA, 1977.

SHAW, M. and HIPGRAVE, T., *Specialist Fostering*, Batsford Academic, 1983.

Chapter 6, pp. 89-97

BERRIDGE, D., and CLEAVER, H., *A Study of Fostering Breakdowns*, Dartington Social Research Unit, 1986.

BRISCOE, C., 'Programme activities in social group work', in MCCAUGHAN, N. ed., *Group work; Learning and Practice*, Allen & Unwin, 1978.

BROWN, A. and CADDICK, B., 'Models of social group work in Britain: a further note', *British Journal of Social Work*, vol. 16, no. 1, 1986, pp. 99-104.

CARTER, W.W., 'Group counselling for adolescent foster children', *Child Care News*, no. 81, December 1968.

DONLEY, K., *Opening New Doors*, British Agencies for Adoption and Fostering, 1981.

EUSTER, S., WARD, V.P., VARNER, J.G. and EUSTER, G., 'Life skills groups for adolescent foster children', *Child Welfare*, vol. LXIII, no. 1, 1984, pp. 27-36.

FORBES, D., 'Recent research in children's social cognition: a brief review', *New Directions for Child Development I*, 1978, pp. 123-7.

HARGRAVE, M.C., and HARGRAVE, G.E., 'Groupwork with pre-adolescents: Theory and Practice', *Child Welfare*, vol. LXII, no. 1, 1983, pp. 31-7.

JEWETT, C., *Helping children cope with separation and loss*, Batsford Academic, 1984.

KAGAN, M.R., and REID, W.J., 'Critical factors in the adoption of emotionally disturbed youths', *Child Welfare*, vol. XLV, no. 1, 1986, pp. 63-73.

LUDLOW, B., and EPSTEIN, N., 'Groups for foster children', *Social Work*, vol. 17, no. 5, 1972, pp. 96-9.

PAGE, R., and CLARK, G.A., *Who Cares?* National Children's Bureau, 1977.

PETERSON, J.B., and STURGIES, C.H., 'Groupwork with adolescents in a public foster care agency' in SCHWARTZ, W. and ZALBA, S., eds., *The Practice of Group Work*, Columbia University Press, 1971.

ROWE, J., CAIN, H., HUNDLEBY, M., and KEANE, A., *Long term foster care*, Batsford/BAAF, 1984.

SELMAN, R., JACQUETTE, D., and LEVIN, D., 'Interpersonal awareness in children: toward an integration of development and child clinical psychology', *American Journal of Orthopsychiatry*, vol. 46, 1977, pp. 74-8.

SULLIVAN, H.S., *The Interpersonal Theory of Psychiatry*, W.W. Norton Company, 1953.

TRISELIOTIS, J., and RUSSELL, J., *Hard to Place: The Outcome of Adoption and Residential Care*, Gower, 1984.

WATERHOUSE, J., 'Groupwork in intermediate treatment', *British Journal of Social Work*, vol. 8, no. 2, 1978, pp. 127-44.

WATSON, K.M., and BOVERMAN, H., 'Pre-adolescent foster children in group discussion', in TOD, R. ed., *Social Work in Foster Care*, Longman, 1971.

WINNICOTT, C., *Child Care and Social Work*, Bookstall Publications, 1970.

WOLKIND, S.N., and RUTTER, M., 'Children who have been "in care": an epidemiological study', *Journal of Child Psychology and Psychiatry*, vol. 14, 1973, pp. 37-105.

YOUNIS, J., and VOLPE, J., 'A relational analysis of children's friendships', *New Directions for Child Development*, I, 1978, pp. 1-22.

Chapter 7, pp. 98-111

ABAFA, *Working with children who are joining new families*, Training Pack, 1977.

FAHLBERG, V., *Helping children when they must move*, BAAF, 1981.

JEWETT, C., *Helping children cope with separation and loss*, Batsford Academic, 1984.

SIM, M., and O'HARA, G., 'Group work with children who are joining new families', *Journal of Adoption and Fostering*, vol. 6, no. 4, 1982, pp. 31-7.

TRISELIOTIS, J., *In search of origins*, RKP, 1973.

Chapter 8, pp. 112-126

BROWN, A., *Groupwork*, Heinemann, 1979.

LINDSEY-SMITH, C., 'The new families project', in TRISELIOTIS, J., ed., *New Developments in Foster Care and Adoption*, 1980.

SHAW, M., and HIPGRAVE, T., *Specialist Fostering*, Batsford Academic, 1983.

TUCKMAN, B.W., 'Developmental sequences in small groups', *Psychological Bulletin 61*, 1965, pp. 384-99.

Chapter 9, pp. 127-140

ADENIJI, F., 'West African fostering: a personal experience', *Foster Care*, no. 33, March 1983, pp. 12-13.

AHMED, S., 'Mek a pickney happy', *Adoption and Fostering*, vol. 93, no. 3, 1978, pp. 5-6.

AHMED, S., 'Selling fostering to the black community', *Community Care*, 6 March 1980, pp. 20-22.

AHMED, S., 'Children in care: the racial dimension in social work assessment', in CHEETHAM, J., JAMES, W., LONEY, M., MAYOR, B. and PRESCOTT, W., eds., *Social and Community Work in Multi-Racial Society: A Reader*, Harper and Row, 1981.

ARNOLD, E., 'Finding black families for black children in Britain', in CHEETHAM, J., ed., *Social Work and Ethnicity*, Allen and Unwin, 1982.

ASSOCIATION OF BLACK SOCIAL WORKERS AND ALLIED PROFESSIONS (ABSWAP), *Black Children in Care: Evidence to the House of Commons Social Services Committee*, 1983.

ASSOCIATION OF BRITISH ADOPTION AND FOSTERING AGENCIES, 'Working with West Indian applicants in fostering and adoption: a discussion paper', in CHEETHAM, J., JAMES, W., LONEY, M., MAYOR, B. and PRESCOTT, W., eds., *Social and Community Work in a Multi-Racial Society: A Reader*, Harper and Row, 1981.

BLACK AND IN CARE STEERING GROUP, *Black and in Care Conference Report*, Children's Legal Centre, 1985.

BRADFORD FOSTERING AND ADOPTION UNIT, 'Families for black children', *Adoption and Fostering*, vol. 9, no. 4, 1985, pp. 5-6.

BROWN, A., *Groupwork*, Heinemann, 1979.

BRUNTON, L. and WELCH, M. 'White agency, black community', *Adoption and Fostering*, vol. 7, no. 2, 1983, pp. 16-18.

CANN, W., 'Meeting the needs of the Asian community', *Adoption and Fostering*, vol. 8, no. 1, 1984, pp. 43-5.

CHEETHAM, J., *Social Work Services for Ethnic Minorities in Britain and the USA*, Department of Social and Administrative Studies, University of Oxford, Dec. 1981.

CHEETHAM, J., 'Introduction', in AHMED, S., CHEETHAM, J. and SMALL, J., eds., *Social Work with Black Children and their Families*, Batsford, 1986.

CHILDREN'S LEGAL CENTRE, 'Placed in a white family – views of young black people', *Childright*, no. 22, November/December 1985, pp. 7-10.

DIVINE, D., 'Defective, hypocritical and patronising research', *Caribbean Times*, no. 104, 1983a.

DIVINE, D., 'Time for decision', *Caribbean Times*, no. 105, 1983b.

DIVINE, D., *Submission to the Jasmine Beckford Enquiry*, June 1985.

FITZGERALD, J., 'Black parents for black children', *Adoption and Fostering*, 103, no. 1, 1981, pp. 10-11.

FRATTER, J., 'Barnardo's black project worker', *Foster Care*, no. 45, March 1986, p. 15.

GAYES, M., 'Soul Kids', *Child Adoption*, 82, no. 4, 1975, pp. 19-21.

GILL, O. and JACKSON, B., *Adoption and Race: Black, Asian and Mixed Race Children in White Families*, Batsford, 1983.

HOUSE OF COMMONS SOCIAL SERVICES COMMITTEE, *Second Report from the Social Services Committee on Children in Care*, vol. I, House of Commons Papers, Session 1983-4, HMSO, 1984.

JAMES, M., 'Finding black families', *Adoption and Fostering*, vol. 98, no. 4, 1979, pp. 5-6.

JAMES, M., 'Finding the families', *Adoption and Fostering*, vol. 103, no. 1, 1981, pp. 11-16.

KNIGHT, L., 'Giving her roots', *Community Care*, 15 June 1977, pp. 18-20.

LAMBETH BLACK CHILDREN'S PROJECT, reported in *Adoption and Fostering*, vol. 7, no. 1, 1983, pp. 6-7.

LINDSAY SMITH, C., 'Black children who wait', *Adoption and Fostering*, vol. 95, no. 1, 1979, pp. 5-6.

LOFTUS, Y., 'Black families and parental access', *Adoption and Fostering*, vol. 10, no. 4, 1986, pp. 26-7.

MAXIMÉ, J.E., 'Some psychological models of self-concept', in AHMED, S., CHEETHAM, J. and SMALL, J., eds., *Social Work with Black Children and their Families*, Batsford, 1986.

MAXIMÉ, J.E., 'Black Like Me' Series (*Workbook One: Black Identity*; *Workbook Two: Black Pioneers*), Emani Publications, 1987.

MENNELL, M., 'The experience of Bradford Social Services Department' in AHMED, S., CHEETHAM, J., and SMALL, J., eds., *Social Work with Black Children and their Families*, Batsford, 1986.

MILLER, D., 'Proud to be black', *Community Care*, 21 February 1985, pp. 18-19.

MULLENDER, A. and MILLER, D., 'The Ebony group: black children in white foster homes', *Adoption and Fostering*, vol. 9, no. 1, 1985, pp. 33-40 and p. 49.

MURRAY, N., 'A basically racist society', *Community Care*, 31 March 1983, pp. 14-16.

NOTTINGHAMSHIRE SOCIAL SERVICES DEPARTMENT, *Report of the Second Ebony Group*, 1986.

PARR, M., quoted in *Black and In Care Conference Report*, Children's Legal Centre, 1985, p. 38.

RANDMAWA, M., 'Prevention and rehabilitation with black families', *Adoption and Fostering*, vol. 9, no. 3, 1985, pp. 42-3.

SCHROEDER, H. and LIGHTFOOT, D., 'Finding black families', *Adoption and Fostering*, vol. 7, no. 1, 1983, pp. 18-21.

SCHROEDER, H., LIGHTFOOT, D. and REES, S., 'Black applicants to Ealing recruitment campaign', *Adoption and Fostering*, vol. 9, no. 2, 1985, pp. 50-3.

SKERRITT, D. and WATKINS, D., 'Positive attitudes in Nottingham', *Caribbean Times*, 23 May 1986.

SMALL, J., 'New Black Families', *Adoption and Fostering*, vol. 6, no. 3, 1982, pp. 35-9.

SMALL, J., 'Policy and practice in transracial placement', in NOTTINGHAMSHIRE COUNTY COUNCIL, *Conference Papers on Transracial Fostering and Adoption*, 1985.

SMALL, J., 'Fostering Understanding' in *Social Services Insight*, 16-23 August, 1986, p. 11 (1986a).

SMALL, J., 'Transracial placements: conflicts and contradictions' in AHMED, S., CHEETHAM, J. and SMALL, J., eds., *Social Work with Black Children and their Families*, Batsford, 1986b.

STEIN, M., 'Protest in care', in JORDAN, B. and PARTON, N., *The Political Dimensions of Social Work*, Basil Blackwell, 1983.

STONE, M., *Ethnic Minority Children in Care: A Report to the Children in Care Panel*, Social Science Research Council, Department of Sociology, University of Surrey, May 1983.

Chapter 10, pp. 143-148

BAILEY, R.L., 'The group method in foster home studies', in *Social Work Practice*, Report of the 90th Annual Forum Conference on Social Welfare, Cleveland, Ohio, 1983.

BROWN, F.G., 'Services to adoptive parents after legal adoption', *Child Welfare*, vol. XXXVIII, 1959, pp. 17-22.

CAUTLEY, P.W., *New Foster Parents*, Human Sciences Press, 1980.

CROWLEY, M., *Preparation for foster care practice – A Survey*, Social Monographs, UEA, 1982.

DOUGLAS, T., *Group Living*, Tavistock, 1986.

DONLEY, K.S., 'Adoption disruptions after legalisation', quoted by Kagan and Reid, op. cit.

FINKELSTEIN, N.E., 'Legal barriers to adoption', Conference held at Parsons Child and Family Centre, Albany, N.Y., Nov. 1982, quoted by Kagan & Reid, op. cit.

GOHROS, H.L., 'A study of the caseworker-adoptive relationship in post-placement services', *Child Welfare*, vol. XLVI, no. 6, 1967, pp. 317-325.

HAZEL, N., *Bridge to Independence*, Blackwell, 1981.

JONES, O.E., 'A study of those who cease to foster', *British Journal of Social Work*, vol. 5, no. 1, 1975, pp. 31-42.

KAGAN, R.M. and REID, W.J., 'Critical factors in the adoption of emotionally disturbed youths', *Child Welfare*, vol. XLV, no. 1, 1986, pp. 63-73.

KIRK, H.D., *Shared Fate*, Free Press, 1964.

MACASKILL, C., *Against the Odds*, BAAF, 1984.

PICTON, C., 'Post-adoption support', *Adoption and Fostering*, vol. 88, no. 2, 1977, pp. 21-5.

SANDLER, I.N., 'Social support resources, stress and maladjustment of poor children', *American Journal of Community Psychology*, vol. 7, 1979, pp. 425-40.

STONE, N.M. and STONE, S.F., 'The prediction of successful foster placement', *Social Casework*, vol. 65, 1983, pp. 11-17.

VEROFF, J., KULKA, R.A. and DOUVAN, E., *Mental Health in America: Patterns of Help-seeking from 1957-1976*, Basic Books, 1981.

YATES, P., *Post-placement support for adoptive families of hard-to-place children*, M.Sc. dissertation, University of Edinburgh, 1985.

Chapter 11, pp. 149-159

CAUTLEY, P.W., *New Foster Parents*, Human Sciences Press, 1980.
HAZEL, N., *A Bridge to Independence*, Blackwell, 1981.

Chapter 12, pp. 160-171

COOPER, J.D., *Patterns of Family Placement*, National Children's Bureau, 1978.
CROWLEY, M., *Preparation for Foster Care Practice – A survey*, Social Work Monograph, University of East Anglia, 1982.
JONES, E.O., 'A study of those who cease to foster', *British Journal of Social Work*, vol. 5, no. 1, 1975, pp. 31-42.

Chapter 14, pp. 182-197

ALTON, H., 'Working with families towards placement', *Community Care*, 29 October 1981, pp. 16-18.
ASSOCIATION OF BLACK SOCIAL WORKERS AND ALLIED PROFESSIONS (ABSWAP), *Black Children in Care: Evidence to the House of Commons Social Services Committee*, 1983.
CHEETHAM, J., *Social Work Services for Ethnic Minorities in Britain and the USA. Final Report of a Study Funded by the DHSS*, Department of Social and Administrative Studies, University of Oxford, December 1981.
CHEETHAM, J., 'Introduction', in AHMED, S., CHEETHAM, J., and SMALL, J., eds., *Social Work with Black Children and Their Families*, Batsford, 1986.
CHILDREN'S LEGAL CENTRE, 'Placed in a white family – views of young black people', *Childright*, no. 22, November/December 1985, pp. 7-10.
CHILDRIGHT, 'New group opposes "black families for black children"', no. 29, July/August 1986, p. 5.
COMMUNITY CARE, 'Transracial adoption: campaign slams blanket bans', 10 July 1986, p. 3.
HOUSE OF COMMONS SOCIAL SERVICES COMMITTEE, *Second Report from the Social Services Committee on Children in Care*, vol. I, House of Commons Papers, Session 1983-4, HMSO, 1984.

KREECH, F., 'An American experience in child care services', in CHEETHAM, J., ed., *Social Work and Ethnicity*, Allen and Unwin, 1982.

MENNELL, M., 'The experience of Bradford Social Services Department', in AHMED, S., CHEETHAM, J. and SMALL, J., eds., *Social Work with Black Children and Their Families*, Batsford, 1986.

MILLER, D., 'Proud to be black', *Community Care*, 21 February 1985, pp. 18-19.

NATIONAL FOSTER CARE ASSOCIATION, *I Like You White, Do You Like Me Black?*, leaflet, undated.

NOTTINGHAMSHIRE SOCIAL SERVICES DEPARTMENT, *Report of the Second Ebony Group*, 1986.

PAYNE, S., *Long Term Placement for the Black Child in Care*, University of East Anglia, Social Work Monograph 15, 1983.

PRYCE, K., 'Problems in minority fostering', *New Community*, vol. 3, 1974, pp. 379-85.

RAYNOR, L., *Adoption of Non-White Children: The Experience of a British Adoption Project*, Allen and Unwin, 1970.

RAYNOR, L., 'Adoption for children with special needs: philosophy and methods', *Social Work Today*, vol. 5, no. 7, 27 June 1974, pp. 194-7.

SMALL, J., 'Policy and practice in transracial placement', in NOTTINGHAMSHIRE COUNTY COUNCIL, *Conference Papers on Transracial Fostering and Adoption*, 1985.

SMITH, R., 'Trans-racial fostering: the debate continues', *Foster Care*, no. 43, October 1985, p. 4.

THORN, J., SKERRITT, D., SMITH, A. and MCGLADE, M., *Report of the First Year of the Black Fostering Project: April 1984 to April 1985*, Nottinghamshire County Council Social Services Department, September 1985.

WHITE, H., *Black Children, White Adopters: An Exploration in Uncertainty*, University of East Anglia, Social Work Monograph 31, 1985.

Author Index

Subject Index